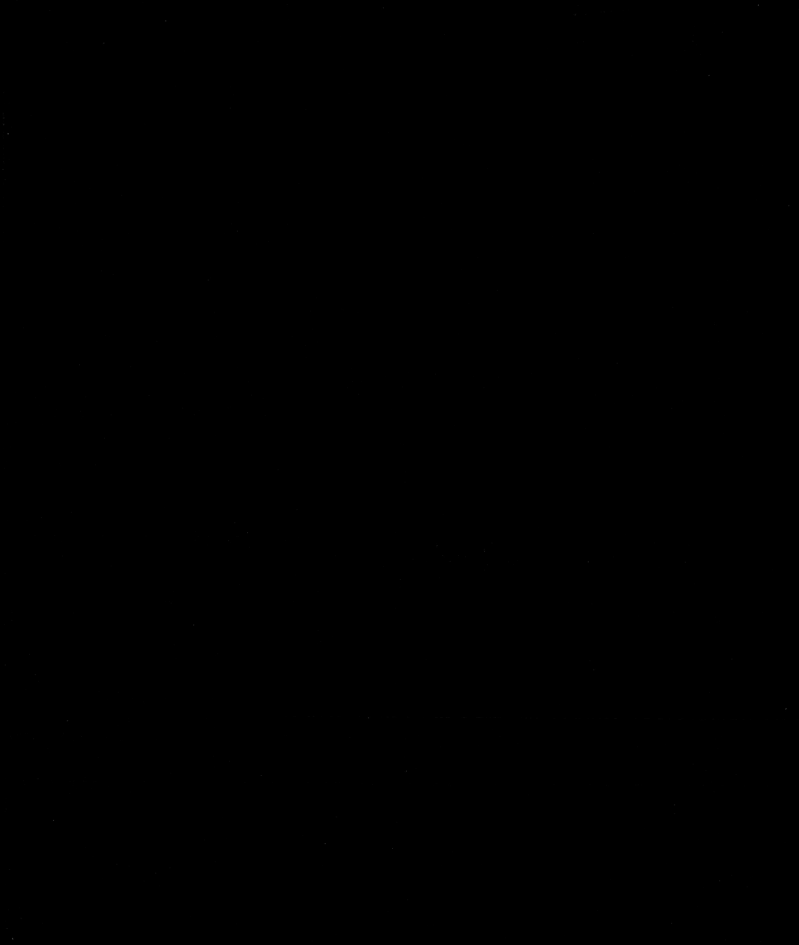

AYRTON SENNA

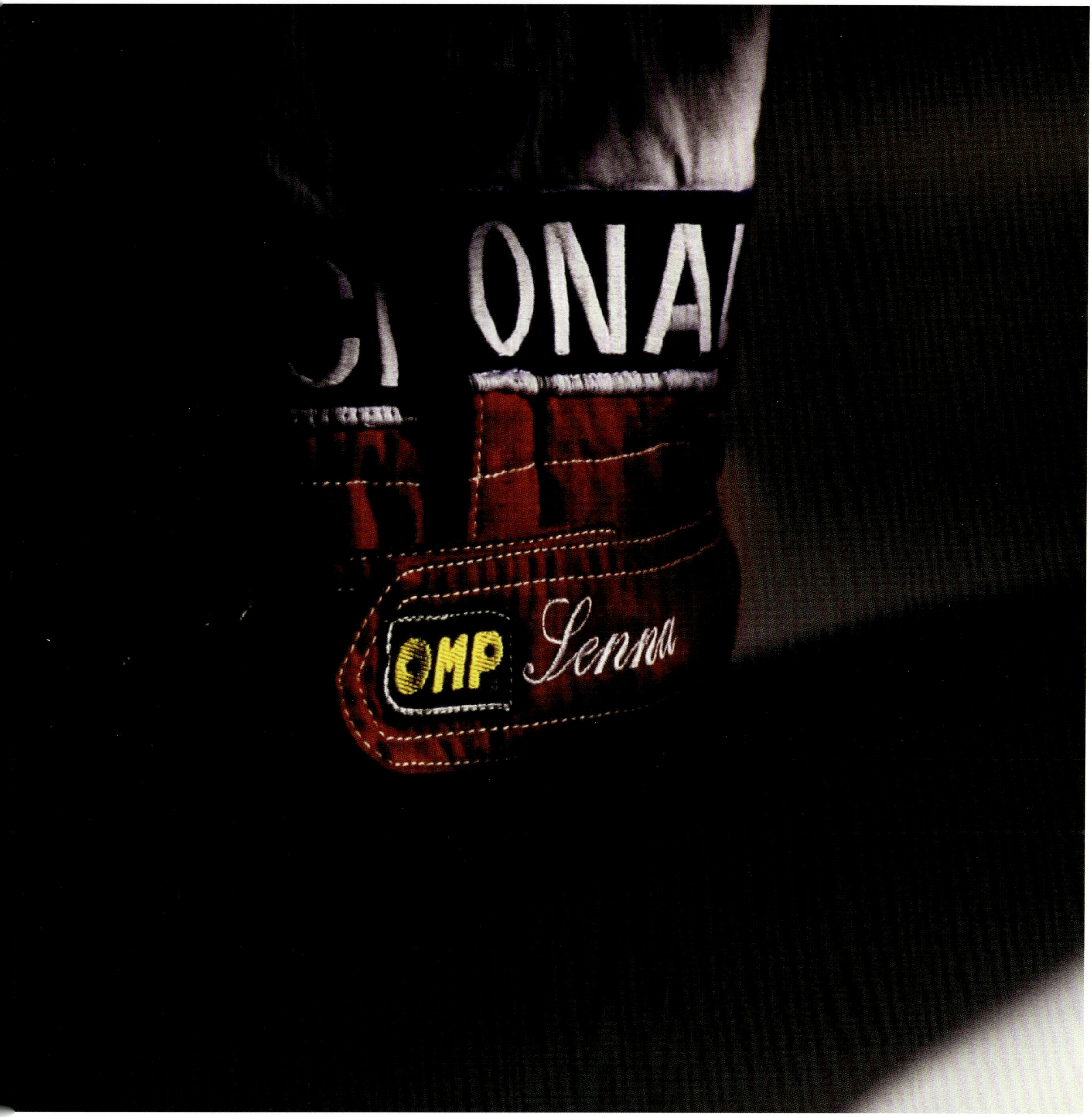
ONA
OMP
Senna

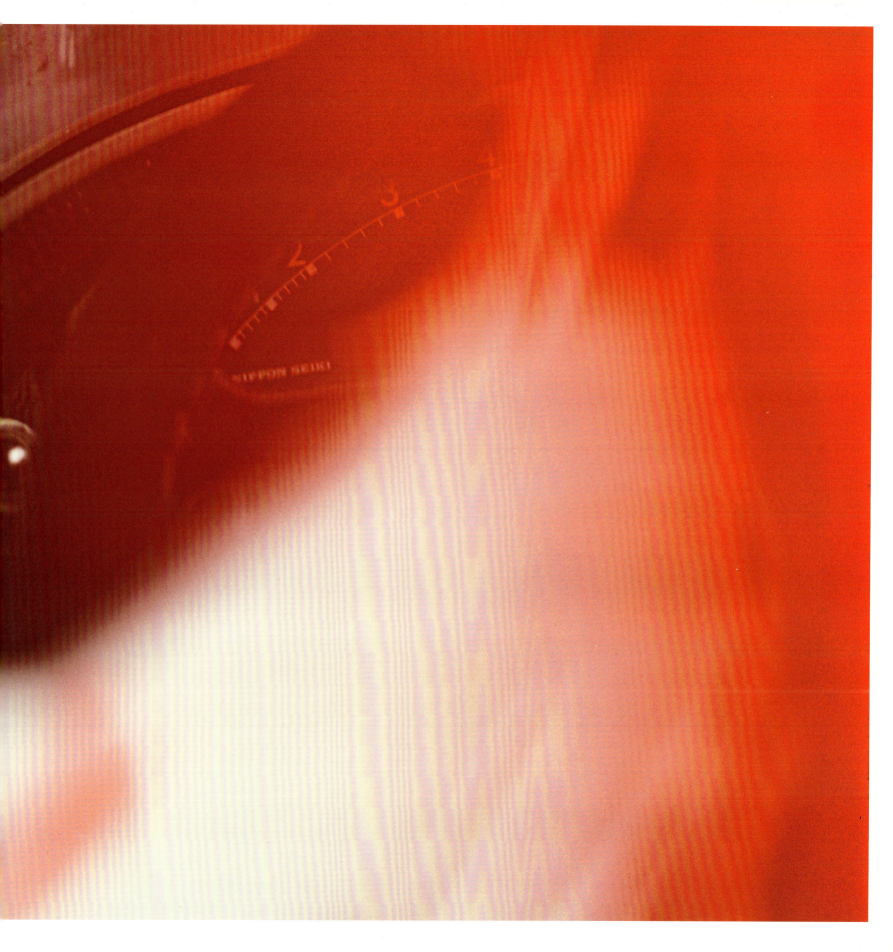

AYRTON SENNA

MAURICE HAMILTON

BLINK
bringing you closer

CONTENTS

FOREWORD

McLaren played such a big part in Ayrton's F1 racing career that he felt the people there were like family. He made many lasting friendships at every level of the team. Ayrton recognised the important part everyone played in victories that meant so much to him; he knew he could not have won races and championships without dedicated team members supporting him all the way.

It's really nice, therefore, that this book pays tribute to my brother by recording many personal memories from the people who mattered to him. He would feel happy and honoured to read the recollections recalling the fun times as well as the difficult periods that affect every racing driver. Certainly, we as a family are very pleased the book has been done in this way.

We are also delighted that *Ayrton Senna* is associated so closely with the Ayrton Senna Foundation. Ayrton had always been worried about Brazil. He felt that he should be an example for his country and he sincerely wanted to help others have the same opportunity that he had in life, not just in racing but in fundamental aspects of everyday life such as education, food and heath.

When Ayrton was in Brazil before the 1994 season started, we had a chat about his dream to do something for Brazilian unprivileged people. He wanted me to help him find the best way forward. We were going to talk about this again when he was back from the first half of the season. Unfortunately, this didn't happen...

But his dream needed to come through and we, the family, decided to open the Foundation. This is our website: http://senna.globo.com/institutoayrtonsenna/ingles/home/index.asp

During the past 20 years, we have been developing social solutions to help the education system in Brazil, by identifying major problems and creating solutions that could be applied at a high level in entire cities and states.

We directly help more than two million children and youngsters and more than 76,000 teachers all over Brazil each year. I'm sure Ayrton would be very proud of our achievements!

As for Ayrton's achievements, they are recorded in this book. We hope you enjoy it. And thank you for helping to support a cause that meant so much to him.

Viviane Lalli

1. NOW AND THEN

Ayrton Senna would have turned 54 on 21 March 2014. His birthday fell on the Friday between the Australian and Malaysian Grands Prix, rounds one and two of the 2014 FIA Formula 1 World Championship.

Had Senna lived, it is interesting to speculate where he might have been; what he might have been doing. Most certainly, his intense focus would have been on the Ayrton Senna Foundation, established in 1994 to provide education for underprivileged children in his native Brazil. Some who worked with Senna even suggest he might have become president of Brazil.

But an interest in racing – the passion that consumed most of his 34 years – would surely have continued. Perhaps he would be a pundit for Rede Globo, the television network that followed Senna religiously throughout his 16 years spent racing beyond Brazil. Maybe he would be promoting the cause of Brazilian drivers; those struggling to enter F1 and those already present.

Had he been in Melbourne, a visit to the Williams team would have been appropriate, not simply because of the presence of Felipe Massa, the only Brazilian in F1 in 2014. Williams would have been a port of call because it's fair to assume Senna would have won the 1994 World Championship (lost by only the narrowest of margins by Senna's successor, Damon Hill). And had Senna remained with Williams, you could argue that another three titles would have come his way. There is a thought, however, that Ayrton might have returned at some stage to the team with whom he enjoyed his greatest success.

Had Senna been in Australia, or any other F1 venue in 2014, it's also safe to imagine that time would have been spent at McLaren. It's the team with which his name will be forever linked whenever Ayrton Senna is revered and remembered – as he is now, on the 20th anniversary of his death on 1 May 1994 at Imola in Italy.

Prior to the fateful move to Williams at the beginning of 1994, McLaren and Senna together won 3 World Championships, 35 Grands Prix and 49 pole positions. While the titles and victories are the end-product of a highly successful driver–team relationship, the last statistic gives a clear indication of an innate speed that made Senna so thrilling to watch.

The bright yellow crash helmet aboard a red and white McLaren became an iconic image representing race car driving at its most dramatic and daring. Driver and car fed off each other to unite in an irresistible combination that remains sharp in the memory decades later. Senna and McLaren: it's a sporting permutation as outstanding as Jim Clark and Lotus, the partnership that dominated the international motor sport landscape as Senna grew up in a wealthy suburb of São Paulo.

Ayrton knew little about Clark when the Scotsman was in his pomp in the sixties because F1 had yet to take serious hold in Brazil, and Senna was only beginning to discover the addictive delight of driving quickly. Milton da Silva (Senna was the maiden name of Ayrton's mother) had built a kart for his four-year-old son, and Ayrton quickly developed a basic control and co-ordination that would never desert him. Senna had his first taste of a proper motor vehicle when he drove a jeep on one of the many farms owned by the family, an early introduction to a clutch and gears being similar to that experienced by Clark when, as a youngster with a comparable and insatiable mechanical curiosity, the shy Scot had been driving tractors on his parents' farm in the early 1940s.

When Clark was killed in April 1968, it brought the same sense of shock and incredulity that would accompany the death of Senna 26 years later. At the time of Clark's fatal accident in a Formula 2 race at Hockenheim, eight-year-old Senna was already thinking about racing a kart – even though he was five years away from the minimum age permitted for competition. That did not prevent him from acquiring an avid desire to prove he was faster than everyone else in minor events on a local track. Meanwhile, at Spa-Francorchamps in distant Europe, Bruce McLaren was scoring the first Grand Prix win for a car bearing a name that Senna would come to know well.

James Hunt (11) makes a slow getaway and is swamped by the Ferraris of Niki Lauda (1) and Clay Regazzoni at the start of the 1976 Brazilian Grand Prix at Interlagos.

By the time Ayrton had reached 13, the image of motor sport itself had been enhanced thanks to Brazil's first World Champion, Emerson Fittipaldi. Senna's talent and F1's popularity at home would develop in preordained tandem. Or, at least, that's how it seemed to Ayrton when he accompanied his father to the first Brazilian Grand Prix at Interlagos in 1973 (there had been a non-championship race the previous year). Fittipaldi, driving for Lotus, thrilled the excitable locals by winning and then delighted Ayrton when Milton introduced his son to the reigning champion.

Fittipaldi returned for his home Grand Prix a year later, to discover he was featuring on billboards throughout São Paulo – the result of rapidly escalating popularity and the desire of his team sponsors to cash in on it.

'Senta a bota, Emerson!' ('Boot it, Emerson!') shouted huge posters depicting a red-and-white F1 car with a driver wearing a black-and-red helmet. This was the McLaren M23, unveiled in March 1973 and now carrying the colours of Marlboro and Texaco, the latter having accompanied Fittipaldi in his recent move from Lotus. The M23 had already proved a winner but 28-year-old Fittipaldi was to move up another gear with three wins (including another emotional victory in Brazil) and the first World Championship for McLaren.

The M23 was still in evidence when Senna and his father made the 45-minute journey from their home to Interlagos to watch qualifying for the 1976 Brazilian Grand Prix. Fittipaldi had left McLaren to run his own team, his place being taken by James Hunt, who proved there was plenty of life left in the McLaren-Ford by putting a revised and developed M23 on pole. The 16-year-old Senna would have been heartened by Fittipaldi taking fifth on the grid, although the penultimate row for the second Copersucar-Fittipaldi of Ingo Hoffman was more indicative of a difficult future for the all-Brazilian team.

More immediately, it would be a disappointing race for the passionate fans, Carlos Pace being the highest-placed Brazilian when he brought his Brabham Alfa Romeo home one lap down in 10th place. The opening round of the season was won by the Ferrari of reigning World Champion Niki Lauda, Hunt having spun off and retired with various mechanical problems to leave Jochen Mass as the sole McLaren representative, in sixth place.

Hunt would go on to take the 1976 title from Lauda at the eleventh hour in a memorable and dramatic season worthy of a film. It was to be the last hurrah for McLaren in that form. By the time Ayrton Senna travelled to Europe for the first time in 1978, McLaren was in decline and due to finish eighth in the championship with not a single victory.

That would have been of little interest to Senna. Now 18 and having won every championship worthy of the name in Brazil, he had come to Italy intent on becoming karting World Champion. This was his first time away from the comforts of a substantial home. It was a culture shock for a quiet young man who spoke only a few words of English and had to get by with a mix of Portuguese and broken Italian while also coming to terms with unfamiliar food. The fact that he endured this without complaint said everything about a determination to prove something to himself on a personal level and to the motor sport world at large when it came to showing how quick he believed himself to be.

Senna had 10 days to become attuned to a DAP kart and work out how he shaped up. There would be no better yardstick than the Englishman, Terry Fullerton, Ayrton's team-mate at DAP and a former World Champion.

Senna's first serious run was at Parma, a tricky circuit about 100 km from Milan. Fullerton had been on track for the best part of a week as he tried different engines. When Senna was finally told to push, he equalled Fullerton's time within 10 laps. Angelo Parrilla owned the team and manufactured the DAP kart. His brother, Achille, overseeing the test, thought his eyes were deceiving him.

Achille Parrilla

Parma is difficult and Senna had not driven before on Bridgestone tyres. He'd been used to Brazilian tyres at home. To drive on Bridgestone soft tyres was not easy, so what he did was astonishing.

Terry Fullerton

He was immediately quick but as a driver he looked a bit raw and obviously not very polished. He did, however, have natural ability. We used to do a lot of testing at Parma. He came down with us; just someone over from Brazil who nobody had heard of and who was paying. People would do that from far-flung places. They'd be reasonably good but you wouldn't think of getting a result out of them – that happened frequently and it still does. But this guy was quick.

This being Italy, word travelled fast that Fullerton was doing lap record times at Parma with some unknown Brazilian sitting two inches off his bumper. It added a frisson of anticipation as the DAP team headed north to race against entries from 12 different countries in the World Championship shoot-out at the Le Mans kart track.

Senna was at a disadvantage because he didn't know how to get the best from his tyres. He won one heat, retired with mechanical trouble from another and finished a very close sixth overall. Senna had arrived knowing nothing about the competition but left Le Mans knowing he was good enough to win. That would do for now. The karting championship would surely come.

Except, it didn't. In a career crammed with success, failing to win the kart world title in several attempts would be a source of constant frustration for a driver measuring achievement by the number of victories and nothing else. He was one of six drivers capable of becoming champion when he tried for the third time in 1980. Senna was regarded as a loner but his rivals knew enough to register two things: they could see how unhappy he was to finish a very close second that year; and they recognised, above all else, that here was a driver who was prodigiously quick.

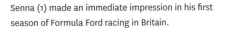
Senna (1) made an immediate impression in his first season of Formula Ford racing in Britain.

Senna (7) dealt with the rough and tumble
of Formula Ford to win 12 races and two
British championships in 1981.

Senna, in turn, could draw some comfort from the sheer pleasure of racing hard in such a simple and pure formula. Some 13 years later, in a post-race interview in Adelaide, immediately after what would turn out to be his final victory, Senna would be asked who was the opponent he had the most satisfaction racing against. Expecting Senna to mention the F1 elite of the day, the audience was surprised by the response:

'Fullerton. Terry Fullerton,' said Senna. 'He was very experienced and I enjoyed very much driving with him because he was fast, he was consistent. He was, for me, a very complete driver. And it was pure driving, pure racing. There wasn't any politics then. No money involved either and I have that as a very good memory.'

Racing in such a simple form was about to become more complicated. Senna moved to England and placed his foot on the lower rung of a ladder that was more clearly defined than it is now. In 1981, progress in single-seater racing began with Formula Ford, stepped up to Formula Ford 2000 and then moved on to Formula 3, each category a step closer to Grand Prix racing.

With that in mind, Senna arrived in the flat expanses of Norfolk; hardly the first choice in mid-winter for a Brazilian but one of the few places to be if you were in England for motor racing rather than the climate, the culture or the countryside. Senna's destination was Van Diemen, a company with a reputation for manufacturing competitive Formula Ford cars and giving opportunities to drivers who could pay but, above all, who could drive. Ayrton's continuing – albeit slightly reluctant – support from his father took care of most of the former. As for the latter, that had yet to be proved. There were plenty of young drivers who were quick in karts. It was by no means a given that they would be winners in single-seaters, particularly in Formula Ford, a category so densely populated with would-be heroes that it could support three separate championships in Britain. Senna entered them all.

Peter Stayner *I was manager at Snetterton, the circuit in Norfolk used by Van Diemen for testing. That's where I first met Ayrton and, of course, I had no idea then that our paths would cross much later when I was working in the marketing department at McLaren. At the time, he was another of the Van Diemen rookies when he came into my office. He was very young, very shy; yet another Brazilian. He didn't speak a great deal of English. I remember it being a cold day – and he hated the cold. We were a sort of clearing house for the good, the bad and the ugly when racing drivers came to Snetterton because we ran seven days a week and, if you had a Van Diemen FF1600, this was where you started.*

Van Diemen was run by Ralph Firman and it became a bit of a joke with Ralph when Ayrton was running because they would ask to keep the circuit open 'just another lap. Just another lap! Ayrton's got to see if this works.' We'd get into half-an-hour overrun and you could tell then that this guy was a bit special because not only was he quick but he was completely focused and dedicated. He would have lived in that car if he could.

Senna's Formula Ford debut for a 12-lap race at Brands Hatch on 1 March 1981 saw a mid-field qualification, occasional wild driving and fifth place. The reporter for *Autosport* magazine may have spelled his name incorrectly but noted: 'Undoubtedly, we shall see more of this young man.' Indeed they would. And sooner than anyone anticipated.

Senna finished third in the next race at Thruxton. An impressive result in itself for a novice in such competitive company, but one that would be superseded in a telling way one week later when he drove away from the field in a wet race at Brands Hatch. Here was the first indication, not just of pure skill but also of an ability learned through karting to search for grip that may not necessarily be on the racing line when the track is treacherous. It was an attribute that, in future years, would leave rivals bemused – and behind.

His confidence growing, Senna went on to win another 11 races, and claim two championships (he barely took part in the third). Then he went home. Ostensibly for good. The Formula Ford world was astounded when, in response to a commentator's question about moving up to F3 for 1982, Senna said: 'No, I finish with racing. I'm going back to Brazil.' Ayrton would later explain his reasoning to Christopher Hilton, the most prolific of Senna's unofficial biographers.

Ayrton Senna

I was very disappointed. One of the main reasons was that, in order to find a sponsor, you need good publicity. That is especially important in Brazil because it is so far away. Of all the Brazilians who have come to England, I was the first to win two championships in the first year. I won 12 races; I qualified on pole 14 or 15 times in 18 races. These were very good results but I couldn't get good press in Brazil, and without that I couldn't find a sponsor. I knew that I needed a sponsor before I could move into Formula 3 and I tried very, very hard. I was competing for space in the newspapers with [Roberto] Moreno and [Raul] Boesel, who were winning in Formula 3, and also Nelson Piquet was winning the World Championship. After all that there was no room [in the papers] for Formula Ford 1600.

There was an additional reason. Ayrton's father was a self-made man running a successful car-components business that, naturally, he wished to pass on to the next generation of his family. The unwritten code of a male-orientated society in Brazil ruled out Viviane, the first-born, and brought the focus on Ayrton rather than his younger brother, Leonardo. Disillusioned over a lack of support for racing from his home country and aware of the unspoken obligation, Senna felt the moment was right to assist in the family business.

Ayrton worked hard from October 1981 to February 1982. But the narcotic influence created by driving a racing car – and driving it well – continued to pull his thoughts towards Europe and the coming season.

Viviane Lalli

My father decided it was time for Ayrton to go back and work in our family business. Although Ayrton's dream was to continue racing and have a career in this path, he didn't complain and went back to Brazil. I'm not sure how long he stayed in Brazil, but we could see he was quite depressed; his 'light' had disappeared. That was when our father and mother realised they needed to accept that their son had a different future than they anticipated and let him go back to Europe to race.

His father understood, as Senna later explained when commenting on text produced by Christopher Hilton. Senna noted on the manuscript: 'He [Senna's father] simply made me free to decide what I wanted to do and, after I decided, we agreed together (father, myself and the family) that this was simply Go! [heavily underlined] and not look back any more, just look ahead. In February [1982] I made up my mind. For sure, without my father's help, life would have been a lot more difficult but we also agreed as a matter of principle that the day I could be in a position [to do it], I would pay back all the investment. That happened when I got to Formula 1.'

There is every chance that Senna would have considered McLaren a future employer when he checked out the F1 landscape in February 1982. In the space of just over 12 months, the team had undergone a major transformation. Struggling to the point of embarrassment in 1980, McLaren had received an ultimatum from Marlboro: either accept change or we take our considerable support elsewhere. It was Hobson's choice.

The management regime formed in the days of Bruce McLaren (who had been killed in a test session at Goodwood in 1970) accepted a take-over by Project Four Racing, an immaculate race team run with distinction in the lower formulae by Ron Dennis. Renamed McLaren International, the revamped organisation changed F1 technical thinking by introducing a carbon-fibre chassis and defying the naysayers in 1981 by winning Grands Prix with this pioneering car.

McLaren were not alone in undergoing an adjustment of title. Senna had previously been known by his surname, da Silva, racing as Ayrton Senna da Silva or, simply, Ayrton da Silva. He decided it was not distinctive enough (da Silva was rather like Smith in Britain or Ferrari in Italy) and, on his return to Europe in early 1982, he simply dropped da Silva and assumed Senna. Other than that, there was to be no difference in his racing persona. The winning would continue.

At Snetterton the previous April, a dominant Formula Ford 1600 performance by Senna in the rain had not gone unnoticed by Dennis Rushen, the owner of Rushen Green Racing, a small team running in Formula Ford 2000 (FF2000). Rushen introduced himself to Senna and offered a drive for £10,000 should the Brazilian be interested in stepping up to FF2000 in 1982. Ten months later, when Senna called Ralph Firman and confirmed that he wished to continue his career after all, a deal was done with Rushen to race a Van Diemen in Britain and in Europe.

Senna on pole at Oulton Park where he won twice en route to the 1982 British Formula Ford 2000 Championship.

Ayrton, leading from the start at
Zandvoort in Holland, won the
1982 European Formula Ford 2000
Championship.

Senna's progress would be watched with interest by Indy Lall, a young mechanic working for Project Four Racing.

Indy Lall

I was running a Brazilian driver, Chico Serra, in F3. Chico was the hotshot at that time and lots of things beckoned for him. Then he had a bad accident at Mallory Park, unfortunately, so that set him back a little bit. But quite openly and freely he spoke a lot about this guy Ayrton Senna and the things he was doing in karting. My first meeting with Ayrton was at an airport somewhere. He seemed very reserved, very shy, but actually quite a warm guy. Not that he was ever flamboyant but you sensed a guard went up until he got to know someone. He was the same age as me and, because we were introduced by Chico, there was an instant understanding and acknowledgement.

When he started doing FF2000, it coincided with the Grands Prix (I had moved up to F1 with McLaren and Ron Dennis) and we started seeing each other a bit more. He was driving for Dennis Rushen, who I knew anyway, so it was quite easy to keep tabs on him. It was very interesting to watch him progress and, I have to say, on every occasion we met, he was very warm, very welcoming; always wanting to know about you. His sincerity and his integrity really stood out and said much about him as a human being. I was not at all surprised at his rise through the ranks.

Senna took his dominance to a new level, winning 21 of the 27 FF2000 races contested, including supporting races at Grands Prix in Belgium, Germany and Austria. The Belgian Grand Prix on 9 May was won by John Watson's McLaren – a result that was completely overshadowed by the death of Gilles Villeneuve during qualifying the previous day.

It is a harsh but true tenet of motor racing that life goes on. Despite the tragedy involving the popular Ferrari driver, the progress was noted of a young FF2000 hotshot with a potentially dramatic flair similar to Villeneuve. It supported the view of two F1 teams that they had been right to make known their interest in the Brazilian with a yellow helmet as distinctive as his driving style.

At a press dinner on the weekend of the Detroit Grand Prix in June, Ron Dennis admitted he had offered to fund Senna's 1983 campaign in F3, with the proviso that he signed an option with McLaren in F1. Dennis looked slightly bemused and marginally impressed when he went on to explain that Senna had appeared unwilling to seize such an opportunity. Senna's view had been that the option would not automatically guarantee a F1 drive and, worse still, it would prevent him from driving for other F1 teams. It was Senna's earnestly articulated view that he would do well enough in F3 to be able to pick and choose the F1 drive that suited him most when the time came.

Ron Dennis *I can't remember exactly what Ayrton was asking for, but I did say to him, 'If you give me an option [for F1], I'll pay for your F3 season.' He made it very apparent – not in a rude way – that he wasn't interested. He felt he had the ability and he wanted to be independent. I didn't exactly like that attitude – but I did respect it. So, when I gave him his first test in the F1 car the following year, I gave him a bit of a comeuppance. I thought: 'Even if you are impressive, I'm not going to tell you.'*

I remember at the test, he came across as very arrogant. He was keen to gain an advantage, asking if he was going to have fresh tyres and also making sure the car wasn't damaged by the other young drivers taking part in the test. He was clearly impressive, but he was still young. You could see in him an 'I'm always right' attitude. He was a very principled individual but, if I'm perfectly honest, he didn't appeal very much at first.

Dennis was not the only one to feel perplexed. Alex Hawkridge, the boss of Toleman, a team relatively new to F1, had also been rebuffed after making a similar offer.

Alex Hawkridge *Ayrton took the view that the car determines your performance so much in F1, whereas in the junior formulae, where the engines, tyres, chassis and power are so similar, individual performance makes you shine. He wanted to prove himself the best – and he was desperately anxious to prove that point to himself as well as everybody else.*

It was kind of ridiculous because he stood out so far as being the exceptional talent of the decade to anybody who bothered to look. And he wasn't just occasionally that; he was systematically that. He qualified fastest, he got the jump at the flag, he got the first corner, he automatically won the race. Since I'd watched Jim Clark in my childhood, nobody had dominated motor racing in the way that he did. It wasn't an aspiration to ever get into Formula 1; it was an ambition to dominate Formula 1. That's all he contemplated.

Twelve wins in the West Surrey Racing Ralt and a dramatic F3 Championship claimed at the final round in 1983. Ayrton's spectacular performances attracted a F1 test drive with Williams (overleaf page 40).

F3 teams may have been in a lower stratosphere to F1, but that did not mean their hunger to succeed was any less intense. F3 team bosses had also noted Senna's potential and, typically for a garrulous Irishman, Eddie Jordan was the first to make an offer, starting with a test drive at Silverstone in June 1982. Jordan made available his Ralt, typical of the F3 genre with its slick tyres and wings; a more powerful version of the FF2000 Van Diemen and, effectively, a Grand Prix car in miniature.

Eddie Jordan

He came with his father on a Wednesday afternoon. We had been racing the previous weekend at the same track and James Weaver had qualified this car on pole with a time of 53.58 seconds and set the fastest lap of the race at 54.40 seconds. Ayrton arrived and did about 30 laps. This was his first outing in a F3 car and he looked amazingly good. He came in and asked for a few adjustments to the car. These were not major changes; just enough for Senna to have the car more to his liking. Then he completed another 10 laps, during which he went faster than James's pole position lap. It's important to remember that qualifying had been done in the morning, when the track and conditions are usually faster, and here was Senna, in a car he didn't know, bettering those times. It was absolutely astonishing.

I could see that he was something very special – only an idiot would have missed that – and I would have done anything to have him on board. In my heart of hearts, though, I knew he probably would not drive for me. At that time, Eddie Jordan Racing lacked the pedigree he was looking for. Normally, I would charge drivers for a test like that but I gave Ayrton a free run. Ayrton appreciated that and we got on well. However, 12 months later, when we were neck-and-neck in arguably one of the greatest F3 championship battles ever, he would hardly speak to me at all.

His FF2000 mission more or less complete, Senna accepted the offer of a drive with the West Surrey Racing team in a non-championship F3 race at Thruxton at the end of the season. He qualified on pole and won by 13 seconds. Senna reached a verbal agreement after the race and signed with West Surrey Racing in January 1983 to contest 20 rounds of the Marlboro British Formula 3 Championship. Fought out on six different circuits, this, as Eddie Jordan noted, would turn out to be a classic confrontation between Senna and Eddie Jordan's similar Ralt, driven by Martin Brundle.

The season initially resembled a rout as Senna won the first nine races. The turning point came in June when Silverstone staged a race that was a round of both the British and the European Championships. With a handy advantage in the British series, and knowing that Brundle needed to stick with it and chase points, Senna opted to enter the European counterpart and enjoy the benefit of the softer tyres from Yokohama that would allow him to win outright. But when Brundle and Jordan changed their minds in the last minute, switched to Yokohama and snatched pole, Senna's weekend began to crumble. In the race itself, he spun twice trying to keep up with Brundle's leading car, finishing the second spin against the barrier and beneath the gaze of the press box.

WE WERE NECK-AND-NECK IN ARGUABLY ONE OF THE GREATEST F3 CHAMPIONSHIP BATTLES EVER.
EDDIE JORDAN

Senna enjoys a win at Silverstone after another close
fight with Martin Brundle (right), his F3 rival in 1983.

When Brundle won three of the next four races, not only was there a shift in the championship momentum but also in the discipline Senna had hitherto exhibited in his driving. With increasing desperation, he left the road a couple of times; at Oulton Park, he landed on top of Brundle's car while trying to overtake.

Eddie Jordan *You could play mind games with Ayrton. We tried to have his car excluded from a couple of races on dubious technicalities and then we would feed non-attributable stories to the motor sport media about the naughty things we were allegedly doing to our car, knowing that Ayrton devoured every written word because he had absolutely nothing else to do with his life at that time. We would employ simple moves to upset him. We knew Ayrton had a thing about being the first in line to go out to practice and he wanted his guys to be first in the queuing for scrutineering each weekend to avoid wasting time. We would arrive early, at about 6.30 a.m., just to be first in the queue. That would irritate him like you wouldn't believe.*

By the time Senna and Brundle reached the final round at Thruxton, there was nothing to choose between them. Senna won the race and, with it, the championship.

That done, it was evident Ayrton was ready for F1. Typically, and rare for a youngster, it was not a case of, 'Would Senna get a drive?' It was a question of, 'Which team will he choose?'

Ron Dennis makes notes during Ayrton's F1 test with McLaren at Silverstone in 1983. They would not work together until 1988.

2. DRIVING A HARD BARGAIN

There were offers of F1 from McLaren, Brabham and Toleman. Of the three, Senna finally chose Toleman, but only after negotiations lasting into the early hours of the morning in Alex Hawkridge's office in Essex.

Alex Hawkridge *The negotiating was completely one-sided. He got what he wanted. Money wasn't a problem at all; it was the conditions of the contract and in particular the buy-out terms of the contract. We were sitting in my office with an open telephone line to his lawyers in Brazil. We were thrashing out the interpretation of the words. He would accept some explanations, he would insist on others being changed. Don't think that he was just a good racing driver – he was good at whatever he did, a man who would excel at anything he put his hand to.*

Ayrton Senna *Toleman was the best offer, the best situation I could have at that time. Toleman was coming up, it was a new team. They really believed I could learn with them and do a good job. They were prepared to commit themselves a lot with me, so I felt that was the right thing.*

Toleman would quickly discover that Senna's view on commitment would be more about him than his team. The first Grand Prix of 1984 was at Jacarepaguá, a flat and fairly unremarkable track on the outskirts of Rio de Janeiro. This being Brazil, Ayrton asked for more than 30 passes to accommodate his family and friends. He was surprised to discover that F1, coming under the increasingly rigorous control of Bernie Ecclestone, did not work like that: he would take the few passes he was given and be thankful.

That misunderstanding may have been resolved with the minimum of discussion, but Senna's handling of a sponsorship issue would cause serious discord within Toleman. Senna's contract allowed him to carry personal sponsorship identification – on the understanding that he would discuss it first with the team. When he appeared with overalls carrying patches for Marlboro and Monroe shock-absorbers, not a word had been mentioned to the team management. Realising Senna needed to be brought to heel, Hawkridge hauled his driver over the coals in private; a belittling and tearful experience for the proud youngster but one that made the point – even though, as McLaren were to discover four years later, Senna would deliberately ignore it as his status and value increased.

For 1984, McLaren's attention was focused on the latest car, the MP4/2 – or, specifically, the engine powering it. The advance of turbo-charging in F1 was such that Ron Dennis and his technical director, John Barnard, had come to the conclusion they needed to commission their own engine rather that rely on customer relationships with either Renault or BMW. In an assertive and pioneering move typical of McLaren, Dennis approached Porsche about designing and building an engine funded by TAG (Techniques d'Avant Garde), a business consortium and team partner. A development car having appeared in the previous year's Dutch Grand Prix, the latest version, MP4/2, incorporated valuable lessons learned during 1983, and was ready in Brazil for the season ahead. The Marlboro McLaren-TAG would win 12 of the 16 races, Niki Lauda taking the championship by half a point from team-mate Alain Prost at the final round in Portugal.

The anomaly of half a point had been created four months earlier when the 1984 Monaco Grand Prix was stopped because of rain, and half-points awarded. This was the sixth race of the season and provided a canvas for Senna's name to shoot to a prominence never anticipated when he had begun his F1 career in Brazil.

THE CAR WAS
IMPOSSIBLE TO
DRIVE AT FIRST.
THERE WAS TOO
MUCH POWER IN
THE WET.
AYRTON SENNA

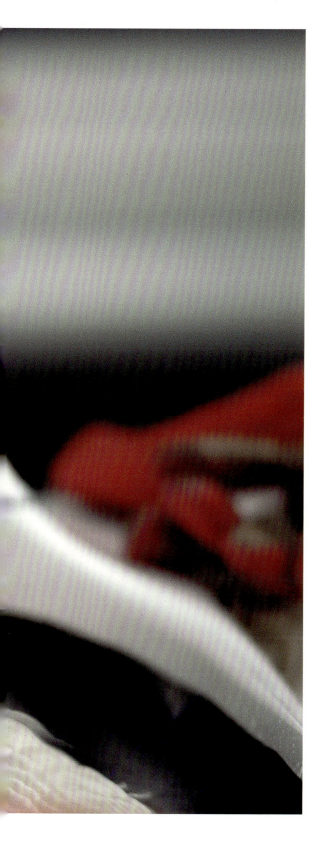

By no stretch of the imagination could the Toleman be referred to as a pace-setter. This was the British team's fourth season in F1 and their humble status when compared with the likes of McLaren and Ferrari was underlined by a tight budget and a car that was pragmatic rather than pretty. Toleman's solution to the need for a turbo was to do a deal with Brian Hart who, despite his talent as an independent engine builder, was similarly restricted by limited funds. Senna found the Toleman heavy and difficult to drive, his first championship point for sixth place in South Africa having come at a price as he was helped, exhausted, from the car. A wet race at Monaco would change all that.

Senna not only qualified (seven drivers failed) for a place on the 20-car grid, he put the white-and-blue car on the seventh row, behind a black Lotus (Elio de Angelis) and ahead of a green Alfa Romeo (Riccardo Patrese). He was destined to move forward quickly in the race when persistent rain tipped the balance in favour of the driver's skill rather than the competitiveness of his car.

Ayrton Senna

The car was impossible to drive at first; there was too much power [in the wet], so I turned the turbo boost down. The more I turned it down, the better the car drove. In the end, I had no boost at all!

By lap 10, he was sixth, gaining two more places by lap 14. Prost, starting from pole, had led the first 10 laps before Nigel Mansell took charge of a Grand Prix for the first time after Prost had been delayed slightly by marshals recovering one of the many damaged cars. Mansell's moment of glory would not last long. Starting lap 16, he lost control as water streamed down the steep hill from Casino Square. The Lotus smacked the barrier, Mansell eventually spinning out of the race a few minutes later. Senna was now third.

The rain seemed to intensify in direct proportion to the narrowing gap between Senna and Lauda. It took just three laps for the Toleman to demote the McLaren and set after Prost, who was 33 seconds ahead. Prost pulled out more than a second on the next lap. It would be the last time he would enjoy such a psychological advantage. As the lap times extended because of the atrocious conditions, the gap to the leader narrowed: 31 seconds at the end of lap 23; 21 seconds at the end of lap 27; 11 seconds at the end of lap 30; 7 seconds at the end of lap 31.

By now, Prost was gesticulating furiously at officials each time he crossed the start/finish line. Jacky Ickx, clerk of the course and a celebrated F1 *regenmeister*, decided enough was enough. The red flag was shown at the end of lap 32. As Prost slowed, Senna stormed out of the spray and drew alongside the McLaren as they crossed the line. Whether he was ahead or not was irrelevant because the final positions would be calculated from the end of the previous lap.

Senna was classified second. Typically, he angrily claimed he would have won the race had it not been stopped. But his disappointment should have been tempered by the thought that the leading pair were being caught by third-placed Stefan Bellof, the young German making the most of his more docile non-turbo Tyrrell-Ford on the slippery streets. And, even if Senna had managed to hold off Bellof, the Toleman was destined not to last, post-race inspection of the car showing serious damage to the right-front suspension after Ayrton had thumped a kerb and briefly become airborne at the harbour chicane.

Nonetheless, a point had been made. Here was a driver of star quality – and now the world knew it. But it would come with baggage – as the Toleman team were about to discover.

Ayrton, on the podium after finishing third at Brands Hatch, hoists the arm of McLaren's Niki Lauda, winner of the 1984 British Grand Prix.

Senna's attraction to leading teams intensified as the season went on and he finished third in the British Grand Prix at Brands Hatch. When JPS Lotus made an offer of $585,000 for 1985, Senna accepted. The problem was, he failed to mention it to Toleman, believing, with an increasingly apparent mix of naivety and arrogance that the team would understand.

The only thing Hawkridge understood was that his three-year contract with Senna included a buy-out clause stipulating a certain sum had to be paid, even before any negotiations took place. Not only had Senna failed to pay, the mismanaged dealing had been exacerbated hugely when Lotus issued a press release revealing their plans for Senna in 1985 and stating rather patronisingly that 'he will, of course, continue to drive for Toleman for the rest of the season'. Hawkridge had other ideas about that.

Alex Hawkridge *I didn't blame Ayrton, or Ayrton's management, for keeping their ears permanently to the ground because everyone does that; it's part of the lifestyle. I didn't even blame Ayrton for deciding his future wasn't within Toleman. He had the right to do that; the clear and express right. What he didn't have the right to do was enter into an agreement with anybody else before he'd advised us and released himself from his contract through an agreed payment. The payment wasn't that large, for Senna it wasn't even an issue, and, in fact, he paid the money that was due. Ayrton was an honest man, genuinely not dishonest – but liable to interpret events liberally.*

That interpretation led to his having no drive in the Italian Grand Prix. Senna was shocked to find, when he arrived at Monza, that Toleman had given his car to Stefan Johansson. The team was upset about how their credibility had been badly damaged by their driver's apparent cavalier attitude. Doubly unfortunate for Senna was the fact that this would be the home Grand Prix for Sergio Tacchini, the Italian sportswear company with whom Ayrton had a personal sponsorship deal. The result was a bemused Brazilian dressed to the nines in an immaculate white tracksuit and wandering around the paddock like a lost soul with nowhere to go and nothing to do. 'I don't want any more aggravation,' he murmured to reporters. 'I just want to go motor racing.'

I DON'T WANT ANY MORE AGGRAVATION. I JUST WANT TO GO MOTOR RACING.
AYRTON SENNA

The final wound came when Johansson finished a strong fourth and would have been on the podium but for a bearing failure. Senna watched the race with TV Globo. Soon, the network would be commentating on a Brazilian driver with a genuine chance of winning a Grand Prix in 1985. But first, Senna and Lotus would have to deal with McLaren, even though the reigning champions were coming under pressure.

Barnard had produced the MP4/2B chassis, which, as its type number suggests, was an improved version of the 1984 McLaren. It seemed adequate enough when Prost crossed the line first in three of the opening four races. But a disqualification because the car was underweight at the end of one of them (the San Marino Grand Prix) meant that Michele Alboreto would head the championship through the middle of the season, more through the steady accumulation of podium finishes than a string of victories for the Ferrari driver. Prost would tip the delicate balance when wins in Britain, Austria and Italy helped the Frenchman towards his first world title. Team-mate Lauda, with just one victory in his final F1 season, finished 10th.

Senna claimed fourth in the championship but the statistic that stood out was his first F1 victory at Estoril in Portugal on 21 April 1985. Typically, he did it with style. Starting with practice.

When Senna set a time more than half a second quicker than anyone else during the first qualifying session, the astonishing lap was attributed to his skill in wet conditions. Opinion changed a day later, however, when he consolidated that performance in the dry and claimed his first of many F1 pole positions.

On race day, the rain returned and showed no sign of letting up. Mansell (Lotus) and Pierluigi Martini (Minardi) spun on the parade lap but, unlike today, there was no doubt that the race would start. Senna was ready and waiting.

Peter Warr (standing, centre, with headset) oversees a test with Ayrton in the Lotus-Renault 97T. Denis Jenkinson (green sweater), the veteran journalist with whom Senna would later discuss Jim Clark, leaves the scene.

He took an immediate lead and was never headed. His view ahead being unimpaired by the spray from other cars may have helped, but he pulverised the opposition from the very start. After 5 laps, Ayrton had caught the backmarkers; after 15 laps he had lapped half a field that was being decimated, seemingly at every turn. By lap 30, seven drivers had spun off and Senna had lapped the sixth-placed McLaren of Lauda. When Alboreto pushed the Lotus of Elio de Angelis down to third place on lap 43, Senna was 58 seconds ahead of the Ferrari. And showing no sign of letting up despite such a clear advantage.

Senna's winning margin at the end of 67 laps was more than a minute. The conditions were so appalling that his fastest lap was 23 seconds slower than pole but, in the process, he had lapped everyone except Alboreto. If Monaco 1984 had been a marker, this was the irrefutable evidence of a sublime talent.

Confidence shored, Senna went on to take pole position at the street races in Monaco and Detroit, as well as Imola, Montreal and Monza. He won at Spa and, a few weeks later, claimed pole for the European Grand Prix. With Lauda unwell and absent for the race at Brands Hatch, his place was taken by John Watson. Having seen Senna from the sidelines, Watson was to have a unique trackside view – an experience – during qualifying.

John Watson

I was on an in-lap going through Dingle Dell and up to Dingle Dell Corner, when I saw this car coming very quickly behind me. Just at the bottom of the dip, Ayrton came through on the inside – I'd left him room. I witnessed visibly and audibly something I had not seen anyone do before in a racing car. It was as if he had four hands and four legs. He was braking, changing down, steering, pumping the throttle and the car appeared to be on that knife edge of being in control and being out of control. It lasted maybe two seconds. Once he had checked the speed of the car and he'd got the right gear, what he was trying to do was maintain [turbo] boost pressure. On a turbo, you lift off and the power goes away very fast. He got to the point of the track where he wanted to make his commitment to the corner. The car was pitched in with an arrogance that made my eyes open wider. Then – hard on the throttle and the thing was driving through the corner. I mean, it was a master controlling a machine. I had never seen a turbo car driven like that. The ability of the brain to separate each component and put them back together with that rhythm and co-ordination – for me it was a remarkable experience; it was a privilege to see.

Senna rounds La Source in the Lotus-Renault 98T on his way to second place in the 1986 Belgian Grand Prix.

A master in control it may have been but the machine could not quite match the consistent pace necessary to defeat either Prost or Alboreto in the championship that year. It would be the same in 1986 even though Senna led the championship briefly after winning in Spain, and again in Detroit. Pole at no less than seven Grands Prix left no doubt about the potential.

The Renault turbo V6 in the back of the Lotus had been losing to the more frugal Honda and TAG engines in an era when fuel capacity was reduced each year (from 220 to 195 litres in 1986). Honda had the upper hand in terms of power but Williams managed to fritter away that advantage by allowing their drivers to fight for the championship at the expense of the team. In a tense three-way fight at the final race in Adelaide, Prost came between Nigel Mansell and Nelson Piquet to claim a surprise third successive driver's championship for McLaren-TAG. Senna came fourth.

He would improve by one place in 1987, finishing behind the all-conquering Williams drivers but ahead of McLaren's Prost and Stefan Johansson. The key was a switch by Lotus from Renault to Honda, although the change of engine brought teething problems that proved costly in the opening races. Senna would lead the championship in June after back-to-back wins on the streets of Monaco and Detroit. Both results gave great personal satisfaction, as he proved in a relaxed post-race question-and-answer session that covered everything from the races to the meaning of life. At times like that, Ayrton would prove to be at his brilliant best off the track as well as on it.

Ayrton Senna

[On driving at Monaco] When the track is very slippery, you feel your heart is here [indicates throat] because, if you like, you are on the edge all the time. No room for a mistake. Then as the day progresses you get into a better rhythm – and then you start losing a bit of power physically, so you have to be careful. The end of a qualifying lap is different. Normally, you give everything you have. Many times, you don't breathe much. Because you can be more sharp with the brake and throttle, you just hold yourself through the corner. So, when you finish the lap, your heart is up there, for sure.

[On winning for the second year in succession in Detroit] My brake pedal was going soft due to too much heat. I decided to slow down by three seconds a lap to hopefully get the pedal back [he was lying second, behind Mansell's Williams but clear of Alboreto's Ferrari]. Eventually, I started to push and Mansell stopped for tyres and I took the lead. At that moment, it was very important for me to know which

pace he was able to run. I had good information from the pits, so I could measure my own pace with his pace on new tyres. I was still pulling away, so I decided to stay out because the brakes were okay and the tyres working well. I just went harder and harder and harder and found I was faster than other people who had stopped for tyres. I had quite a big gap and decided to take a chance, keep up my average and not motivate the others to stay strong. My only concern was towards the end. If the rubber became too thin, I would lose grip or some pressure but I didn't have any information on that. But then I had been able to save the tyres when going slow because of the soft brake pedal. That helped me decide to take a chance. I tried to keep a minute gap in case I had to make a stop 10 laps from the end. I didn't need to stop. It paid off.

Senna's ability to analyse everything around him while driving flat out had impressed Peter Warr, as recorded in the Lotus team manager's biography, *Team Lotus: My view from the pit wall*:

'Ayrton had flawless balance in low-grip conditions and a surreal feel for the very limit in changing track conditions. Also uncanny was his apparent total recall of everything that was happening in the cockpit. It is one of the hardest things to grasp that at the very edge of the performance envelope in the car, he could separate so completely the physical requirements of driving the car from his mental processes. Time and again he would astound the engineers by telling them exactly what was happening with the chassis or the engine before they had seen the computer printouts. He could drive, talk, analyse the behaviour of the car and recall what the instrument readouts showed, all at the same time.

'For the 1986 Spanish Grand Prix, we found ourselves at the new circuit of Jerez. There had been no prior testing. On Friday, Ayrton qualified with a time of 1min 21.605s. The next best time was in the 1m 23s bracket. The next day, the track was slower and his best lap was in the 1m 22s – ahead of everyone else. When I said he could get out of the car because no one was going to beat his Friday time, he said he wanted to wait in the car. About 15 minutes later, he appeared to be asleep in the cockpit. With about 10 minutes to go, he said he wanted to go out again. When I said there was no point, he replied: 'I've just been going round the lap in my head and I now know I can do a 21.9. I've worked out where I can save a few tenths.' We thought: why not? So we let him go. His time? 1m 21.924s.'

Meanwhile, Senna had been in contact with Honda, prior to the Japanese company joining Lotus for 1987.

Ayrton Senna *The first time I had any contact with Honda was at the end of 1985. It was not even with the Honda people themselves, but somebody in-between and it was regardless at the time of whether I was going to stay with Lotus for 1987. But when I started to decide whether to be with Lotus or somewhere else in 1987 then I investigated quite a lot what the possibilities were and the options. That, of course, included the engine side. I went to Japan for the first time in December 1986. There was, at that time, the possibility of going to McLaren but it didn't happen.*

It would, however, 'happen' in 1988. It was not a coincidence that Honda also left Lotus for McLaren. But Senna's decision came after a typically lengthy discussion, albeit settled in an unorthodox way.

Ron Dennis

Ayrton was renting a house in Esher, which was 15 minutes' drive from our factory at that stage and, when we were negotiating, the meetings always seemed to be midday and it was a series of days going backwards and forwards. I would go back and do other things and he would sit for 24 hours deciding how he was going to position himself for the next round of negotiations.

How we structured the contract regarding the non-fiscal matters was quickly established; it was the fiscal issue that was difficult. We came to a rock and a hard place over half a million dollars. It's wrong to make it seem as though half a million dollars was trivial but it became a point of principle about who was actually going to win that vast part of the negotiations. In essence, he was thinking, 'I am going to drive for McLaren, even if I have to drive for half a million less.' I was saying, 'I am going to give him the half million extra because we want him to drive for McLaren.' So, neither of us were concerned about this additional money but more about losing the last part of the negotiations.

The moment came when I suggested, because we both had a very firm position, we break the deadlock by tossing a coin. Ayrton's English was not very good at this stage and the concept of tossing a coin was something that did not happen in Brazil. It took a while to explain and then, of course, it got quite serious. We realised we should be very clear about the rules. I had to draw a picture of a head and a tail and explain that the coin could not land on its side; it had to be flat. We went over the rules several times to make sure there was no misunderstanding and then discussed who was going to toss the coin and whether we were going to catch it or let it fall to the ground. We then had a couple of practice runs.

I had a very small office with a brown shagpile carpet, which was not a particularly good surface for the coin to land on. We tossed the coin and, amazingly, it rolled under the curtain. As we jumped up, I said, 'Remember, if it's on its side, it doesn't count,' because we could not see it. He lifted the corner of the curtain – and the coin was flat. It had rolled off the side of the curtain and onto the flooring. It was absolutely flat. I had won and it was only later that I realised this was a three-year contract. So, in fact, we had thrown a coin for 1.5 million dollars. I doubt anyone has ever done that before. It makes it sound as though we were disrespectful of money, but it is nothing to do with that. This was simply a way to break the deadlock.

Senna and McLaren were about to move into a dramatic era of competition, camaraderie and conflict, some of which would need to be settled by more than the flick of a coin.

3. SLIPPING INTO THE RED AND WHITE

IT WAS WHEN A RACING DRIVER
MOVED FROM BEING AN ARTIST
TO MORE OF A SCIENTIST.
NEIL OATLEY

Senna's first appearance in the cockpit of a McLaren was an unofficial one. The absence of photographers and the media was fortuitous as Ayrton, wearing bright yellow overalls carrying identification for Camel cigarettes, slid into a red-and-white McLaren bearing allegiance to Marlboro.

Officially, the 1987 season had come to an end a few minutes before as Gerhard Berger's Ferrari finished the Australian Grand Prix a few car lengths ahead of Senna's Lotus-Honda. Ayrton had been the only driver capable of taking the fight to Ferrari but his efforts were to be made worthless in terms of results when a protest by the Benetton team had the Lotus disqualified because of over-size brake ducts.

Under normal circumstances, Senna would have been upset by his team's mistake. But the Lotus part of his life was now history. If Ayrton was annoyed, he didn't show it as he immediately switched his thoughts to the season ahead and walked a few doors down the pit lane to McLaren's garage.

The mood there was subdued by both cars retiring with brake trouble; clearly a sensitive issue on the street circuit in Adelaide. But the atmosphere was lifted when Senna appeared unexpectedly as packing up began at the end of a long season. Among the McLaren crew were Neil Oatley, race engineer to Alain Prost, and Indy Lall, a mechanic on Prost's car and well known to Senna.

Indy Lall

After the race, Ayrton came straight over to us. He wanted to sit in the car. It seems surreal because, of course, that sort of thing would never happen now. Ayrton was like a kid, wanting to play with his new toy. That's all there was to it because he couldn't do anything; we weren't going anywhere to test; we were just packing to come home. But he couldn't wait to sit in the car. Having known him for so many years and watched him progress into F1 and win races, we were the same age and I was learning as much as he was learning. It was an absolutely amazing feeling for me to have him come to race in our team.

Neil Oatley

I had never met Ayrton until the moment he came into our garage. He more or less came straight in and sat in the car. My memory is that he didn't fit very well because that car was actually quite small. We had Alain and Stefan [Johansson] driving for us and the cockpit was, of course, based on when Niki [Lauda] had been our driver. We hadn't really changed much in the chassis from those days. Ayrton's legs were hard against the steering rack. That MP4/3 then became a mule for the Honda engine during the winter.

The mule would quickly become the unloved member of the team once the McLaren-Honda MP4/4 made its debut just a couple of weeks before the start of the 1988 season.

Opposite: Senna brought a relentless work ethic to McLaren that surprised everyone, including his team-mate in the other car.

Indy Lall — *I was running the test team and we had a horrendous time with this hybrid 1987 MP4/3 car with a Honda engine during tests in Brazil. The final test before the first race of the season was held at Imola [in Italy]. While we were there with this awful car, the race team arrived with MP4/4 – and it just looked the bollocks. We were knackered and we were sort of shovelled into the corner because Ayrton and Alain didn't want to know about the old car any more – and you can't blame them. But it gives me goosebumps to this day when I think about what happened next. The MP4/4 went on track and the lap times just went quicker and quicker and quicker. It was getting dark – and Ayrton didn't want to stop. It was an absolutely amazing experience.*

Neil Oatley — *When Ayrton came to see us in the pits in Adelaide, he had been quite relaxed. But when he first tested the car, he was very intense and you could tell he was raising the game to a higher level. He already had a very good relationship with [Osamu] Goto [Head of Honda's F1 engineering programme] and the senior Honda engineers. The effort Ayrton put in with Honda was way beyond what our drivers – and anyone else in the pit lane – were doing at that time.*

The turbo engines were much more complicated than the normally aspirated engines. We were also going more into the electronics and the fuelling, all of which were very important for driveability and therefore of great interest to Senna. The amount

of time he put in at the circuit with the Honda guys just to try and get all those little bits to come together was quite a revelation. Alain was obviously very dedicated, but this pushed things to another level and opened his eyes to where he had to go.

Ayrton was evolving the technique he had started with the 1984 Toleman-Hart, a car that must have been more difficult to drive and didn't have the back-up Honda had to fix any problems. I'm sure Ayrton learned a lot from the Renault experience [with Lotus] because their commitment was immense at that time. But Honda quickly caught up and passed that level. Ayrton grew up with that and evolved how he went motor racing at this next stage of his career.

Ayrton worked hard on his relationship with the Honda personnel, particularly Osamu Goto (overleaf page 76).

We were also at a time when telemetry and data recording were just coming in as a regular part of motor racing. Rather than having a casual conversation with the driver in the motorhome once practice or the race had finished, we had these TV screens and the driver could look intensely at what was happening. This was something new for everyone and Ayrton was at the vanguard of that; it was right up his street. Working with Honda, he could make the engine the way he wanted to drive it.

This sort of stuff was new to the engineers as well. We'd operated on a fairly intuitive level until the early '80s and suddenly you had all this data that helped an understanding of why certain things were happening. No longer were you relying on subjective comment from the driver that could lead you to be working under a misapprehension. Now you had data to either corroborate what they were saying, or show it was different to what they thought.

It was when a racing driver moved from being an artist to more of a scientist. This was when we began to see a different style of driver than we had been used to. You could see what the driver was trying to do and how the car was responding when, say, he came on the throttle and you could actually measure how you were improving it. Having a driver with the intelligence and intensity of Ayrton was a tremendous boon when progressing the car.

The days were over when the drivers would disappear from the track after practice had finished. Ayrton would spend a few hours with the Honda guys – probably spend more time with the engine

people than the chassis people, in fact – because this was all a novelty. You'd see him sitting in the car before qualifying, playing the laps through his mind. He'd sit with his eyes closed, totally focussed on what he wanted to do with his next set of tyres. He had done this with other teams but it was something we had never seen at such a level of intensity.

The whole thing worked for Ayrton because he also had a good understanding of Japanese culture and he could develop relationships, particularly with Goto. You got the impression that Goto was well in with the McLaren camp and not particularly interested in what was going on at Lotus-Honda in 1988.

McLaren MP4/4: arguably one of
the most elegant F1 cars of all time;
certainly, one of the most successful.

Osamu Goto

Ayrton wanted to understand everything about the engineering side. He would take a very logical approach and he respected any technical input about the car, not just the engine. Compared to Prost, he had less experience and so he was always trying to make up for that by using engineering information to help understand how to control and how to drive the car. Compared to Lotus, it was different at McLaren because we became more involved with Senna. We liked his driving style and his approach, not pushing too much initially and waiting for the right moment to make an unexpected lap time. This was appreciated and therefore we started talking more and more to him.

He would give information about his lap – every lap and not just a fast qualifying lap. He could talk about what was happening on a corner entry and on the exit. His explanation of one lap was quite long! He remembered so many details; so many clues about how to improve and go faster. It was very impressive.

With a single exception, no one other than McLaren would win a race in 1988. In one of the most remarkable seasons, either before or since, McLaren claimed 15 of the 16 races. It would have been a clean sweep had Senna not become involved in a collision while lapping a backmarker in the Italian Grand Prix at Monza.

Ayrton started from pole no fewer than 13 times, won 8 races and his first World Championship. But, Monza apart, it had not been a year without incident.

Senna's season had got off to an unfortunate start in his home Grand Prix. Having secured pole position, the gear linkage became deranged on the parade lap, forcing Ayrton to complete the lap of Jacarepaguá stuck in first gear. Rather than enter the pits and miss the start, Ayrton cleverly assumed his position on the grid – and then stuck his arm in the air to force a restart.

The rules in 1988 were not as sharply defined under such circumstances as they are today. Senna was able to have his car wheeled to the pit lane where, as he suspected, it was ascertained the problem could not be fixed immediately, so he elected to take the start in the spare car. It was probably not allowed, but would officials dare to stop Senna in front of his passionate supporters? Having worked his way up to sixth place by half-distance, the spectacular effort would come to nothing when the tardy display of a black flag signalled his disqualification for failing to start in his designated race car. All of this would have the added frustration of being played out before Ayrton's family, as his sister Viviane Lalli and her daughter Bianca took the opportunity to visit their home Grand Prix.

I REALISED AT THAT MOMENT THAT I WAS WELL OVER SOMETHING CONSCIOUS. I DROVE BACK SLOWLY TO THE PITS AND SAID TO MYSELF THAT I SHOULDN'T GO OUT ANY MORE THAT DAY.
AYRTON SENNA

Bianca Lalli

Obviously, we knew he was the same person and he treated us the same way as usual, but he couldn't pay us a lot of attention when we were at the track because he was focused on what he was doing. He was always worried and serious during the Grands Prix. Basically, we would see him going in and out of the car and sometimes making a joke with us. And that would be it. I wasn't surprised about his intensity because, for me, he was the Ayrton I knew, but more focused and more worried about his job. F1 is not easy, and we could feel that as well. You don't have space to stand and you are always feeling that you are in the wrong place. This was Ayrton's life and we were watching from the side. But, deep down, we knew he was the same person.

The Brazilian race was won by Prost. When Senna made up for that with a pole-to-chequered-flag victory at Imola, he knew he was on course to close down the championship gap to Prost by dominating the next race at Monaco, a favourite of his and the scene of an emotional win in the yellow Lotus-Honda twelve months before. Senna did not simply take pole; he destroyed the opposition in the process.

Neil Oatley

I was running Alain's car. Alain had got down to a 1 minute 26.9 seconds. And then Ayrton produced a 24.4 seconds. Alain improved to a 25.4 seconds – but then Ayrton did a 23.9 seconds. I remember a kind of ghostly look came over Alain's face; he just couldn't understand how or where Ayrton's time had come from. It illustrated that, despite all the technology, the driver could still make quite a big difference.

That astonishing lap would ascend into legend, particularly when Senna later thought about how it had been done. Ayrton had struck up a strong and trustworthy relationship with motor sport journalist, Russell Bulgin. The Englishman would sadly succumb to cancer in 2002 at the age of 43, but not before he had made his mark as a truly imaginative and gifted writer. Much of his talent had been spent capitalising on the friendship with Senna and a unique series of interviews. In one, recorded at a Silverstone test on 27 June 1990, Ayrton talked about the qualifying lap at Monaco two years before.

Ayrton Senna

In qualifying, we used race tyres, not qualifying tyres, so you could do many laps. I remember starting; going quicker and quicker. I was on pole by a few tenths [of a second] and then by half-a-second, and then almost a second and then over a second. I was just ... going, more and more and there was a stage when I was two seconds quicker than anybody else, including my team-mate with the same equipment.

I realised at that moment – suddenly! [snaps fingers] – that I was well over something conscious. Monaco is small and narrow and at that moment I had the feeling that I was in a tunnel; the circuit was just a tunnel for me. It was going-going-going and within the physical limit of the circuit. It was like I was on rails. Of course, I wasn't on rails.

Then, suddenly, I realised it was too much; I slowed down, I drove back slowly to the pits and said to myself that I shouldn't go out any more that day. Because for that moment, I was vulnerable for extending my own limits, and the car's limits: limits that I never touch before. It was something that I was not – not that I was not in control – but I was not aware, exactly of what was going on. I was just going-going-going. An amazing experience.

Senna's experience would be of an altogether different kind the following day at Monaco in 1988. The anticipated threat from Prost would be heavily compromised when Alain missed a gear at the start and dropped to third behind a Ferrari, leaving Ayrton with a clear track on which to display his magic. When Prost finally moved into second place on lap 54, Senna was 49 seconds – or three quarters of a lap – ahead.

Aware that he had no chance of catching his team-mate in the remaining 24 laps, Alain played a psychological card by setting the fastest lap of the race. Senna replied but, rather than make a mistake when pushing close to the limit, there would be a tiny lapse in judgement when he backed off in response to Prost doing the same.

Ayrton brushed a barrier at Portier, an innocuous right-hander he had been through at speed 66 times that afternoon. The error was small but the effect was devastating as the McLaren was flicked across the road and into the waiting metal barrier on the opposite side. Senna was out of the race. Prost was heading for victory and a 15-point lead over Ayrton in the championship (in 1988, points were awarded 9, 6, 4, 3, 2, 1).

For Senna, the only good thing about crashing at Portier was having his apartment just a few minutes' walk away. He quickly retreated there and, for several hours, remained out of contact with the team. This was very frustrating for everyone, particularly the pit crew who did not know the detail of what had happened. Mark Hannawin was one of Ayrton's mechanics.

Senna's mastery of Monaco sometimes exceeded even his own extremely high expectations.

Ayrton's reaction to a driving error during the 1988
Monaco Grand Prix gave Ron Dennis a revealing insight to
his driver's uncompromising pursuit of perfection.

Mark Hannawin

We obviously knew something had happened because he hadn't come round. But we just didn't know what had gone wrong. You wonder if something was loose or broken; you ask yourself: 'Did I tighten this; did I do that; did something come loose?' We had absolutely no idea because there was no contact with Ayrton. We flew back to England that night, had the next day off and went into work on the Tuesday. That's when we found out he'd just tapped the barrier. But it's a long time to wait to discover you'd done nothing wrong.

Ron Dennis

His post-accident emotion was pure anger with himself; I have never seen nor heard him more frustrated and angry. He knew that he had effectively lost concentration and made a fundamental error. He could not cope with it at all. When he finally composed himself, he was very negative about his performance and very apologetic to the team.

Ayrton was completely dedicated, completely focussed, derived tremendous satisfaction and uplifting emotional experiences out of racing and winning races. He was unique in the sense of how much of an adrenalin rush he used to get, not just from winning, but from fantastic qualifying laps and, of course, world championships. It was always an emotional rollercoaster for him.

That rollercoaster ride would continue through the next four races when he won two of them ahead of Prost but, by finishing second to Alain in the other two, the Frenchman's points advantage remained at 15. The gap would shrink to six points when Senna won the following race at Silverstone and Prost failed to finish. Or, to be precise, chose not to finish.

The British Grand Prix was run in appalling conditions. Prost dropped from 4th on the grid to 11th on the opening lap and spent the next 23 laps slipping further back as he battled spray and back markers. The French press had their knives at the ready when Prost pulled into the pits and abandoned the race.

Alain Prost *When there's a lot of standing water on the track, I don't like it. I have never pretended I do. I can be quick in the rain, especially if I'm on my own. At the start at Silverstone, I was simply swamped in the middle of the field. Okay, it's the same for everybody but when you are flat out on the straight, you see absolutely nothing at all. Nothing. I'm not worried about driving on a slippery track surface. That's all part of the business we're in. But when you're driving blind; that's not motor racing in my book.*

Senna won the race by more than 20 seconds from Nigel Mansell's Williams; two brave performances in the circumstances. By winning the next three races, Senna finally moved to the head of the championship table – and remained there despite the collision with the backmarker at the next race at Monza, Prost having been eliminated with a rare engine failure. That said, there were only three points separating the McLaren drivers with four races to go. The next one in Portugal would bring the first public indication of a major strain on the thin veneer of harmony between the drivers.

It is difficult to say whether or not a new chassis for Alain made a difference, either psychologically or in terms of performance, but the race weekend at Estoril was to bring an upturn in fortune for Prost, starting with the second qualifying session on Saturday afternoon.

The report in *Autocourse* lays out the interesting details: 'Out early in the [60-minute] session, Alain improved on his Friday [qualifying] time to take provisional pole. Senna knocked a couple of hundredths off that and went quicker still about 10 minutes later. Then Prost, running his second set of tyres, returned to trim another half second off his rival's time. And it looked easy. In fact, he said he was not quite ready since the tyres had not warmed up sufficiently but, when you see a clear lap at this place, you have to go for it.

Senna's precision on the track was matched by his recall when
in the pits. Engineer Steve Nichols makes notes on his clipboard
while more fuel is added for another run at Monza.

'Then Prost pulled his best move yet. With practice having been stopped to allow the recovery of a wayward Coloni, he nipped back to the motorhome and changed out of his overalls. While Senna waited to go out on his second set, knowing that the track would be busy during the final 15 minutes, he had the unnerving sight of Prost nonchalantly hanging around the garage, almost daring the Brazilian to take pole.

'The closest he got was on his sixth flying lap. An electrical fault had caused the instrument warning lights to flash on and off and that, coupled with constant problems with traffic, meant that Senna lost his rhythm, the tyres lost their edge and Ayrton lost pole for only the third time this season. He kept his enthusiasm for his team-mate's achievement under polite control.'

With the McLarens starting from the front row (for the ninth time in 1988), Senna was aware that his three-point advantage in the championship was under serious threat. Prost would start from the inside for the run down to the first corner, a fast right-hander. Senna would have the advantage of the clean side of the track.

Autocourse takes up the story: 'Senna made the better start but Prost was moving across [from right to left] and showing every intention of taking the line into the first corner. It was Senna, however, who turned in first but this no-holds-barred struggle proved to be for nothing. A collision between cars behind them brought out the red flag.

'Now we had a repeat of the first start – only this time Prost ran Senna that bit closer to the edge. The Brazilian chopped across his team-mate to take the lead. That, it seemed, would be the last Prost would see of McLaren number 12.

'We didn't bargain for a very determined former World Champion. And neither, come to that, did Senna. Prost was in no mood to play second fiddle. He made a faster exit through the final comer and, coming along the pit straight, Prost darted out of Senna's slipstream and began to pull alongside. Senna then introduced the first hint of desperation seen all year.

'He suddenly swerved right, forcing Prost to run close to the wall and mechanics to pull back their signalling boards for fear of having them ripped out of their hands. Prost's car skipped sideways over a bump and Senna wisely allowed him some more room. All of this, of course, was at around 180 mph.

Getting edgy. Prost defends his lead into the first corner
during the opening laps of the Portuguese Grand Prix.

'Rather than be intimidated, Prost kept coming and, once ahead, he showed his displeasure by easing Senna back across to the left-hand side of the track, the better to take the line and the lead into the first corner. Prost would not be troubled by Senna for the rest of the afternoon.'

In the motorhome afterwards, they had a brief but tense discussion. Facing the media not long after, Prost said: 'It was very dangerous. I could do nothing. If I'd backed off I might have hit his rear wheel. If we have to take risks like that to settle the World Championship … well, I don't care about it. If he wants the championship that badly, he can have it.' Senna, for his part, said he had been angry after Prost had almost forced him onto the grass at the start.

Prost continued his confident form by dominating the Spanish Grand Prix, but a truly storming drive, after stalling on pole

at Suzuka, saw Senna come back from 14th to win the race in Japan and, with it, the title. A win for Prost in the final race in Australia would actually bring his total to 105 points (compared to Senna's 94 overall) but the convoluted points scoring structure meant each driver could count only his best 11 results from the 16 races.

Having won the title, Senna went back to Brazil, where his parents, sister Viviane and family knew exactly how much this meant to Ayrton.

Viviane Lalli *This was one of the most important moments of his career. There had been many expectations and doubts about him – about his real talent – but the championship ended those doubts. He felt like a burden had finally been lifted from his shoulders. He was extremely happy and proud of his achievements.*

Ayrton's eyes betray the intense focus that went into every second in the cockpit.

The relationship between Prost and Senna, respectful and businesslike, was put under strain going into 1989.

Prost and Senna had finished the season without further potentially serious incidents on track but the Frenchman's measured words in Portugal, spoken through gritted teeth, had made it clear their tenuous relationship was never far from breaking down.

Alain Prost *I have to say that the '88 season was not that bad when I look back on it now, although I did feel the difference in the team at the beginning of that year when Ayrton came. But I was not unhappy. I think it was the way to go: to have a new start in the team with Ayrton and Honda engines.*

I had a meeting with Honda at the end of the year in Geneva. I remember like it was yesterday, meeting Mr Kawamoto and three other people from Honda. We said we had a tough year in 1988 but we did not have any problems with Ayrton that year. There were tough moments like Portugal; that happens. He won one more race [eight to seven] but, if you remember, I could have won Hungary when I overtook him and then went a bit wide. I started from seventh; he was on pole. That's part of the game.

But at this meeting at the end of the year, I said to Honda: 'I don't want to enter into any technical consideration, but when you see an engine arriving at the track that is special for Ayrton, then, psychologically, that is not easy. He has won the championship and I have come second and we had a good year, but I want to have the same treatment for 1989.'

But the fight from the beginning of 1989 was to be worse – much, much worse.

I HAVE TO SAY THAT THE '88 SEASON WAS NOT THAT BAD WHEN I LOOK BACK ON IT NOW, ALTHOUGH I DID FEEL THE DIFFERENCE IN THE TEAM AT THE BEGINNING OF THAT YEAR WHEN AYRTON CAME.
ALAIN PROST

4. WHEN THE LAUGHING HAD TO STOP

The 1989 season looked promising from Senna's point of view: he would now feel settled in the team; turbo-charged engines and a limit on fuel capacity were gone (the latter robbing the more stealthy Prost of an ace card); having won the title, Ayrton would be more chilled and therefore even quicker.

Ayrton would indeed be faster. But the combination of F1 and relaxation would continue to be anathema for a man whose desire to be the best – and be recognised as the best – raged more fiercely than ever before. The previous year was history; 1989 would be another story that, in Senna's view, required just one ending.

The beginning was not ideal when it came to his peace of mind. Making a slow start from pole in Brazil, Ayrton's challenge got no further than the first corner at Jacarepaguá where a pincer movement brought contact and a dislodged nose on the MP4/5. After a stop for a replacement and several more pit visits, the race became no more than a test session. Senna was classified 11th, two laps behind the winning Ferrari of Nigel Mansell. Prost finished second after running most of the race without a clutch, a problem that precluded a second pit stop for fresh tyres but did not prevent the accumulation of a handy six points.

Events in Rio had been among the familiar woes expected in racing. What happened next in Italy would also, at first glance, appear to be no more than the routine cut and thrust of F1. But, within McLaren, the San Marino Grand Prix would provide a deeply significant turning point in the relationship between their two drivers.

At first, the weekend seemed pleasantly routine. McLaren had carried out an eight-day test at Imola, trying four different engine specifications in a bid to make the Honda V10 more powerful and driveable. One engine had done 2,500 miles; another had run for 720 miles without regular attention.

These were depressing facts for the opposition to swallow, particularly when Senna and Prost were almost a second and a half quicker than anyone else during qualifying. After the seemingly false promise of Rio, it was back to the old routine as Senna (starting from pole) and Prost then lapped the entire field and ran the race as they pleased. Or as Senna pleased, to be precise.

The first hint of dissension came when a sullen Prost received his trophy on the podium, made his excuses and left the circuit without attending the post-race press conference. He mumbled something to the French media about an 'accord' having been breached. Rivals, searching for any chink in McLaren's seemingly impenetrable armour, could only hope this breach, whatever it was, would be of some consequence.

For the moment, however, the news of a possible rift at McLaren took a back seat to the story of Gerhard Berger's remarkable survival after his Ferrari had hit the wall at more than 160 mph and instantly become an inferno. The Austrian had left the road at Tamburello, a fast left-hander that would be forever associated with an outcome much more tragic and far-reaching five years later.

In the days immediately after Imola, details of the dissent began to emerge; details that differed depending which McLaren driver was speaking. The common factor was a private arrangement between the two. In the light of Senna's first-corner collision in Rio, it had been agreed that the driver making the best start would be untroubled by the other through Tosa, the first slow corner at Imola.

That seemed to work out fine when Senna had a clean start and held a 2.7-second lead over Prost after three laps. Then Berger crashed and the race was stopped.

IT WAS BUILDING UP STEAM
AND WAS ABOUT TO GET OUT
OF HAND. ALAIN AND AYRTON
WERE PERFECTLY MATCHED
IN TERMS OF DEVIOUSNESS.
RON DENNIS

Heading for trouble. Prost leads
Senna at the re-start of the San
Marino Grand Prix at Imola.

At the restart, Prost made the better getaway and led the field through Tamburello and on towards Tosa. Assuming both the racing line and the thought that Ayrton would adhere to Alain's concept of the agreement, Prost was startled when his team-mate rushed into the available space on the inside before taking the corner and a lead he would never relinquish. It had looked innocent enough from the outside. But within the cockpit of McLaren number 2, the driver was seething.

While Alain was at first reluctant to say much beyond the breaking of an accord, Ayrton was soon prepared to elaborate.

Ayrton Senna *I think there is a divergence of interpretation of the concept of this accord and then, above all, a disproportion between the consequences of the overtaking move and his [Prost's] reaction after it. At the restart, he got away a little better than me but I was immediately on his tail to profit from the suction. I thus gathered speed and I made my move well before the braking area. My overtaking move was begun, in my opinion, well before the first corner and, as a result, outside the terms of our accord.*

What should I have done? Lift off in a straight line because I was going faster than him? We're in races, yes or no? And I braked later than him; I was better placed; that's all. Never have I wished to betray our accord; not for one second did I think it was dishonest. The agreement has always been that no overtaking manoeuvre would happen under braking at the first corner. My overtaking was initiated by slipstreaming Prost during the straight and by the first corner we were side-by-side.

Meanwhile, McLaren had previously arranged for both drivers to attend a test at Pembrey in South Wales.

Neil Oatley *It was unusual for us to have both drivers at a test at this stage of the season. There was quite a fast left-hander at Pembrey, just after the area where we parked the trucks on a former runway at the edge of the track – there were no garages or anything like that. This was a two-day test but, because it was just after Imola, Ron flew down to Swansea airport to speak to both the drivers and try and patch the relationship up. We didn't know much more than that.*

Ron Dennis

I flew in by helicopter. The team at that time had a minibus with two bench seats facing each other and we sat there. I was so angry. It was understandable that the media were making a big story out of this – it's what they love to do – but I felt it was not the sort of thing we needed to be dealing with. Without doubt, it was building up steam and was about to get out of hand. I'd thought this through. Alain and Ayrton were perfectly matched in terms of deviousness; they would play their national press; they'd go to Honda; do lots of things. The psychology was: if I can be the bad guy and make them hostile to me, then they won't be hostile to each other. They would join forces and agree that I was being tough. I'm no pussycat and, in the end, I had them both in tears. It was challenging, but it was the way to handle it. Everyone went off for about 15 minutes, collected themselves, and everything was okay. My message, as always, had been that no driver is bigger than the team.

Neil Oatley

I think we were the first people to test at Pembrey at a time when it was still run by the local council, and before the BARC [British Automobile Racing Club] got their hands on the circuit. It was a novelty to have F1 cars there and the local council were bending over backwards to help. There was a fish-and-chip van, which would normally have been sitting on the sea front or wherever, and the council arranged for it to come and do lunch for us. A friend of mine was a lecturer at the Swansea Institute and he came down for the day. He ended up having lunch with us on a picnic bench and table. Ayrton was sitting next to him, passing the time of day and chatting while they munched fish and chips. It was a surreal scene, thinking back on it now.

The McLaren crew would go from one extreme to the other when they moved from the flat airfield in Carmarthenshire to the steep excesses of Monaco. If Ron Dennis had hoped his meeting with the drivers in Wales would ensure a reasonable working agreement and an end to the discussion, at least in public, Prost was to roll a smoking bomb under the door of the media centre in Monaco.

In an interview with the French sports paper *L'Equipe*, Prost said: 'I do not wish to drag McLaren into difficulties caused by the behaviour of Senna. McLaren has always been loyal to me. At a level of technical discussion, I shall not close the door completely but for the rest I no longer wish to have any business with him. I appreciate honesty and he is not honest.'

Senna arrived in the Monaco paddock to find just one topic of conversation: Prost's interview in *L'Equipe*. His response was straightforward and final.

Ayrton Senna

I am persuaded that in acting like that, Alain wanted to implicate me, make me carry the can, make me culpable, in a phrase: put pressure on me. Since that day [publication of the interview], it's finished. I don't want to hear any more talk about that guy.

Neil Oatley

From that moment, there was no conversation between the two drivers for the rest of the season. In the debrief room, there would be the two drivers, Gordon Murray [technical chief] and two engineers – Steve Nichols, who was engineering Ayrton, and myself. Ayrton would ask me questions about what our car was doing and Alain would ask Steve. Occasionally they could manage a 'Hello' but that was the limit of their communication. Apart from that, the rest of the team was immune to what was going on between the two drivers although I'm sure Ron was getting it in the ear from both of them. It didn't really affect the rest of the team; the intensity of their relationship didn't spill over. As far as we were concerned, it was a good fight for the championship because, fortunately, we were reasonably dominant.

Gordon Murray

There had been an atmosphere in McLaren where people were heading off with their own race engineers and doing a debrief and then choosing tyres and stuff. I insisted that the debrief was done with both race engineers present and both drivers present and that I heard everything that was going on. They might not have liked it, but there was very little chat between the two of them at this point in any case. But at least everything was out in the open. I used to threaten them with all sorts of retribution if I caught them talking separately with their engineers. We managed to download all the information. There might have been – and I'm sure there was – psychological double and triple bluffing, but that's always been there.

More than a second faster than Prost in qualifying at Monaco, Senna started from pole and led all the way to win by just under a minute and give McLaren another one-two. But Senna's second victory in the principality was not as straightforward as it looked.

Neil Oatley

Ayrton was leading by a reasonable distance when he lost first and second gears. Rather than back off to look after the gearbox, he was actually trying to make sure his lap times did not suggest he had a problem. He was driving every lap like a qualifying lap while partly crippled by having two gears missing – which, at Monaco, is quite a problem. He felt that if he backed off it would have inspired Alain to start pushing.

Senna moved to the head of the championship after starting from pole and winning in Mexico. A week later, on 3 June 1989, at the United States Grand Prix in Phoenix, he claimed his 34th pole position to beat the record of the late Jim Clark. This would mean a great deal to Ayrton, since he recognised the Scotsman's reputation even though he had never seen the former World Champion race. Senna was acutely aware of the widely held respect for Clark as both a naturally gifted driver and a decent man.

AYRTON WAS SITTING NEXT TO HIM,
PASSING THE TIME OF DAY AND CHATTING
WHILE THEY MUNCHED FISH AND CHIPS.
IT WAS A SURREAL SCENE.
NEIL OATLEY

On a charter flight in 1984, when there had been no seat allocation on the return to London from the Portuguese Grand Prix, Senna had taken the opportunity to sit beside Denis Jenkinson, then 63 and considered the doyen of motor sport journalists. Jenkinson, who did not hand out praise lightly, had made no secret of his admiration for Clark and found himself being quizzed by Senna over precisely what made Clark special, not simply as a driver but as a sportsman who had the love and respect of his team. Whatever Jenkinson said clearly had an effect, judging by Ayrton's response on 3 June to his new record.

Ayrton Senna

I feel rather light-headed, with no weight on my shoulders now that I have established the new record. I take the record from Jim Clark, a man I never saw racing but who by his results was obviously a very special driver. It is a big moment for me.

Unfortunately for Ayrton, that special moment would not be made complete by victory the following day. He dominated the race until an electrical problem sent him into the pits after 34 laps. Prost assumed the lead and won, a result that put him back in charge of the championship and momentarily eased the Frenchman's concern in Mexico that some Honda engines appeared to be more equal that others.

Ayrton contemplates the effect of his retirement from the British Grand Prix at Silverstone.

Indy Lall

I clearly remember Alain making a strong point that he felt Ayrton was getting preferential treatment from Honda. Ron [Dennis] came close to taking it personally because he had always made a point of both drivers being treated the same. He'd say: 'If there's only one of anything, it doesn't get used. It's as simple as that.' It was always like that, right from the start. In those days, we would take up to 16 engines to a race weekend. Ron got all the engines in the garage and said to Alain: 'Choose what you want.' He made the point right there. End of argument.

If Ayrton thought the retirement on the streets of Phoenix was bad, worse was to come in Canada two weeks later. Neither McLaren won; neither McLaren finished!

Prost retired with a front suspension failure after just two laps but Senna's frustration would be more extreme. In a race of changing conditions, Ayrton would show his now familiar exquisite skill, particularly when dancing the slick-shod McLaren on a damp track in between showers. Then, having dropped back due to a tyre-change, he would produce a full-on attack to retake the lead. No one could touch him. With an advantage of around half a minute, he backed off slightly. Then Senna's Honda V10 blew up just as he passed the pits with 3 of the 69 laps to go. It was the first engine failure for longer than Ayrton cared to remember. And it had to happen now. Prost continued to lead the championship.

It was to be a bad omen; Senna also retired from the next two races, Prost winning them both. The momentum would swing back and forth as the season moved into its second half. With five races remaining, Prost had 62 points; Senna 51. However, with only a driver's best 11 results (from 16) counting towards the championship, Prost was worse off, having scored ten times compared to Senna's six. But the mathematics would move in Alain's favour when Ayrton failed to finish in Italy and Portugal, the latter retirement being as controversial as they come and having nothing to do with a failure on his car. Well, not directly.

Ayrton was on pole (almost as a matter of course) with Berger's Ferrari alongside, Nigel Mansell's Ferrari sharing row two with Alain. These four would be the major players in this 71-lap drama acted out on a hot and sunny afternoon in late September.

The Ferraris actually gave the McLarens a hard time during the first phase but the trouble began when Mansell relinquished the lead to stop for fresh tyres at the end of lap 39. He overshot and broke the rules by reversing out of the Benetton pit box, where he had ended up.

From that point on, Mansell was technically disqualified. But he rejoined and quickly worked his way into third, behind Senna and Berger's leading Ferrari (these two having already made their stops). The race stewards informed Ferrari of Mansell's disqualification; the black flag, accompanied by Mansell's number, was displayed at the start/finish line. Mansell later claimed he didn't see the black flag because he was running in close company with Senna, the pair of them passing the pits at 170 mph and heading into the sun.

By the time Mansell had passed the pits three times, the McLaren management realised he was not stopping; worse still, Ayrton was fighting for the championship and engaging in battle with a driver who had no right to be there. No one needed reminding of the potential calamity given the track record of these two when running in close company.

As Senna rushed past the pits at the start of lap 49, Ron Dennis got on the radio and advised Senna to ignore Mansell. Ayrton, unable to understand the message, asked for it to be repeated. As he did so, Mansell swept from behind the McLaren and was beginning to draw alongside when Senna turned in to Estoril's very quick first corner. The right-rear of the McLaren struck the left-front of the Ferrari. Suspensions buckled instantly and both cars spun into the gravel and out of the race.

Neither driver was hurt. Mansell vacated the Ferrari and headed for the pits. For ten seconds or more, Senna stood, hands on top of the crash barrier, staring straight ahead. He may have been able to keep his emotions under control at that point but all hell broke loose when he eventually got back to the McLaren garage.

Ayrton's frustration over the collision was exacerbated by his pit stop having taken 12.5 seconds; twice as long as the norm at that time. The mechanics, led by Neil Trundle, knew the reason, even if Ayrton did not.

Neil Trundle

It was one of those few occasions when we saw the other side of Ayrton. When he came in for that pit stop, we already knew we had a problem with the rear wheels and the screws coming loose. We should have told Ayrton, but we didn't. We agreed that, in the pit stop, if we took the wheel off and the screws had eaten into the wheel, we knew how to do the screws before putting the wheel back on. It was down to the guy on the wheel to take it off and look. We ripped the wheel off, put the new wheel on – but the guy did a double take to check everything was okay, and it was a slow stop as a result.

When Ayrton got back to the garage, he was shaking with anger. And I mean shaking. He grabbed me by the shirt and said: 'Who put the f***ing right-rear on?' I couldn't tell him the story at that moment of how we'd agreed to check the screws; that it was done for all the right reasons because he could have lost the wheel. We should have told him beforehand, of course. I was very upset. Someone had a word with him and he apologised at dinner that night. He had a fiery temper, but I'm glad to say we didn't see it that often.

Neil Oatley *That was probably the first time I saw Ayrton really lose it when he came back to the garage. He was angry with the team because we hadn't told him Mansell wasn't really in that position. But we'd made a slow pit stop and I think, because it had happened in a previous race and it was the same wheel, he had convinced himself it was a conspiracy by one of Alain's mechanics. No way that would have happened – but it gave you a clue about his mindset.*

Senna's mood would not have been helped when he checked the monitors and saw that Prost had finished second to extend his lead of the championship. With three races remaining, Ayrton had to win two of them and finish second in the other. He said he would keep fighting. No one, least of all Prost, doubted that for a single second.

Helped in part by the exclusion of Mansell (for the Estoril black flag incident) from the next race at Jerez, Ayrton led from start to finish, Alain finishing a circumspect third in a Spanish Grand Prix completely free from drama. The penultimate round in Japan would make up for that in spades.

The McLaren drivers laid their cards on the table in their individual way, Prost's strategy being marginally the more telling, certainly the more surprising, when it came to predicting the outcome at Suzuka.

Ayrton Senna *I have nothing to lose. I will drive as fast as I can to win. It is the way I like to drive. I like the challenge of racing to win. It's something that stimulates me.*

Alain Prost *A lot of times, if you remember, last year and this, I opened the door and, if I did not open the door, we would have crashed. I will not do that this time.*

On-car camera technology had been improving over the years and the F1 media were grateful for it during qualifying on the Saturday afternoon at the wonderful Suzuka track. The pictures from across Senna's right shoulder were truly mesmerising as he hustled the MP4/5 and Honda V10 to the absolute maximum in the 98 seconds it took him to stun the opposition into total submission. Pole number 41. Now for the race.

Ayrton's frustration would very occasionally spill over into the garage.

Prost boxed clever during the warm-up on race morning, setting up his car for better straight-line speed. Senna chose not to reduce his wing angle. With the pair of red-and-white McLarens starting from the front row, we were set fair for an incredible contest. *Autocourse* takes up the story:

'At the pre-race briefing, the drivers were warned that the start would be a quick one, the gap between the red and the green lights being shorter than usual because of the sloping grid. It was very quick; maybe no more than two seconds. Prost was ready for it. Senna was not.

'Having made the best start, Prost was determined to capitalise on it. At the end of the first lap he was 1.4 seconds ahead. Lap two and the gap was 2.2 seconds. At the end of lap five, the lead had stretched to 3.8 seconds.

'Every lap, Senna would set his personal best but, today, Prost was proving to be even quicker. It was a major turnaround, one that said quite clearly that Alain Prost was determined actually to take the title from Ayrton Senna.

'A locked right-front wheel going into the hairpin gave some indication of Senna's best effort on lap 12. Even so, that only reduced the gap to 4.7 seconds and, shortly afterwards, Prost went faster still.' The pit stops came and went, Senna's taking 9.6 seconds compared to 7.8 seconds for Prost.'

Neil Oatley *Alain had pulled something like five seconds in front and it looked like he was fairly comfortable, but then Ayrton started to pull it back. The gap went from 4.6 seconds to 1.8 seconds in a ten-lap period.*

Senna was right with Prost but, because of the Frenchman's straight-line advantage, the final chicane remained one of the few – if not the only – place where Ayrton might try to overtake. After all, he had to win this race to retain the title.

On the 47th lap, Senna made a lunge for the lead with a move that placed heavy reliance on Prost giving way. On previous occasions, maybe. But not on 22 October 1989. Inevitably, perhaps, the two cars collided and came to a rather pathetic halt, locked together in the middle of the track.

Neil Oatley *Standing in the pits and seeing both cars go off was the worst nightmare. Alain is not a dirty driver but on that occasion he, let's say … didn't do it very well!*

Prost vacated his car immediately. But Senna had to keep going and his method of rejoining via the escape road would be the cause of a controversial exclusion. At which point, Alain Prost became the 1989 World Champion. Meanwhile, in the pits, the McLaren crew – among them Mark Hannawin – were trying to work out what was going on.

Mark Hannawin *We saw it on the big screen opposite the pits and we thought both cars had stopped. Then we heard Ron shouting: 'Ayrton is coming in!' We instinctively went to change the nose but the Japanese marshals were trying to stop us because they had some sort of message to say Senna should not be continuing. These marshals were pretty determined and they had to be thrown to one side by a couple of our big guys so that we could change the nose. I was at the front of the car and I remember looking at Ayrton; his eyes were like golf balls, just staring straight ahead. As he shot out of the pits, everyone said: 'We're going to win this!' Ayrton did catch up, overtook a Benetton and crossed the line first. Then all hell seemed to break loose.*

THE CHICANE WAS THE ONLY PLACE WHERE I COULD OVERTAKE AND SOMEBODY WHO SHOULDN'T HAVE BEEN THERE JUST CLOSED THE DOOR.
AYRTON SENNA

The victory was eventually given to Alessandro Nannini in a Benetton-Ford. Nannini, although delighted, admitted this was no way to score his first (and only) win. And neither was it an acceptable way for the championship to end.

Neither Senna nor Ron Dennis would let the matter rest. An appeal was launched and recriminations flew. Prost said Senna had gone too far in every sense. Senna was convinced he was in the right and could not bring himself to mention his team-mate's name.

Ayrton Senna

The chicane was the only place where I could overtake and somebody who shouldn't have been there just closed the door and that was that.

Jean-Marie Balestre, the president of the FIA (Fédération Internationale de l'Automobile) laid the blame squarely at Senna's door, his inappropriate and pompous pronouncement being greeted with dismay by many, including Max Mosley, due to become President of FISA (Fédération Internationale du Sport Automobile, the FIA's sporting arm) two years later.

Max Mosley

When Senna and Prost had the coming together, Balestre just fixed the whole thing [by influencing the stewards]. I was outraged. It went against all my instincts. I would never do that. People used to think I spoke to the stewards; I never did in my entire 18 years [as president]. This wasn't Balestre's role. Balestre was the legislature, not the judiciary. He didn't understand about the separation of powers.

On the Friday following the Japanese Grand Prix, McLaren arrived at the FIA Court of Appeal in Paris in the belief that they were dealing solely with the question of Senna having missed the chicane as he rejoined immediately after the collision. To their amazement and dismay, the McLaren legal team found an entirely new series of allegations were being levelled against Senna, questioning his driving ethics and much else besides. Despite a robust defence, McLaren were not surprised when the appeal was rejected. Worse still, a $100,000 fine and a six-month suspended ban were added by the FIA.

Collision of wills. Senna and Prost come to a halt after disputing the lead at Suzuka.

Senna and Ron Dennis were angered by Ayrton's exclusion from first place in Japan (left). Rain would not dilute his resolve at the start of the final race in Australia.

A press conference in London, followed by another on Dennis's arrival in Australia for the final race, made it clear the McLaren boss thought the exclusion (based on Senna's manner of rejoining the track) was unjust. In an emotional statement appealing for the media's assistance, Senna vowed that he would fight on.

Ayrton Senna

This is totally unacceptable because they are treating me like a criminal. It is both unfair and unrealistic. Yes I do feel threatened by their actions and I did consider retiring from racing over the past few days. So many things have gone through my mind, but I am a professional and the values I have are stronger than many people's.

I never caused the incident. I am aggressive, determined and dedicated to my profession and on many occasions have worried about giving the audience a good performance. But the version that has been given to you about the Suzuka incidents, the logistics, the exit and everything, presented me as being an irresponsible lunatic who was breaking the rules.

It would have been some comfort to end such a controversial few weeks on a victorious note but comfort was not appropriate – in any sense – on race day in Adelaide. Torrential rain, which never looked like easing, caused the start to be delayed by 30 minutes. During this time, debate raged over whether or not the race should be held in conditions verging on suicidal.

The officials remained resolute. Ayrton climbed into his car (on pole, of course) to demonstrate that he was willing to race even if others were not. In the end, all 26 drivers went to the grid. Prost, starting alongside Senna on the front row, completed one lap and returned to the pits. Senna, meanwhile, was in a race of his own.

On the second lap, the first of what would be many incidents caused the race to be stopped and restarted. Once more, Senna disappeared into the distance, the rest struggling in impossible spray. Ayrton, despite spinning more than once, would soon face the same challenge as he began to lap the backmarkers. Powering down the back straight on lap 14, Senna pulled out to overtake a Lotus – and ran straight into the back of a Brabham totally obscured by the spray. Both Senna and Martin Brundle, driver of the Brabham, were fortunate to escape unhurt.

Mark Hannawin

In the pit stops for that race, I was working on the left-front. Ayrton came in and everyone immediately sprang into action, changing wheels. But we just stood there doing nothing – because there was no left-front corner on the car. It had been ripped off in the accident. Ayrton was sitting in the car, smiling, as he watched the guys change the other three wheels by automatic reaction and then stand back and realise what had happened. Ayrton knew he wasn't going anywhere in a hurry.

The race would eventually be stopped after more than half the field had been wiped out. It was a shocking piece of race management by a governing body that, only a matter of days before, had been preaching to Senna about safety on track.

Ayrton returned to Brazil to consider his future. In one of his many discussions with journalist Russell Bulgin, Senna explained why Brazil meant so much to him.

Ayrton Senna

My family are my life; they are my point of reference. It's always important to come back to a reference point when you go all over the world. Otherwise you may lose your way.

Bianca Lalli

We knew that he was very annoyed. I think it was the first time we noticed he was very quiet and … sad, really. He felt that his beliefs were being challenged and people didn't understand what he was doing. Above all, he felt that people were taking advantage of him; they weren't doing what he thought was right. He was a very straight person and, for him – and for our family as a whole – it is very annoying and disappointing when people do things wrong. The things that were happening at that time weren't fair and he really felt that.

Rather than 'lose his way', Senna's period of reflection at home appeared to sharpen his understanding to a potentially damaging degree. On 10 November 1989, he held a press conference in São Paulo and stated bluntly that the FISA and Balestre had manipulated the outcome of the 1989 championship in Prost's favour. This, predictably, did not go down well in Paris.

The FIA issued another of many statements, this one declaring that if Senna did not retract allegations about how the championship had been settled and pay his $100,000 fine by 15 February 1990, he would not be given a Superlicence. The laughing had stopped. Clearly, it was going to be a long winter.

5. 1990: ONE ALL

An information sheet issued by Honda Marlboro McLaren prior to the first Grand Prix of the 1990 season listed 'The Investors'. Philip Morris, through its Marlboro brand, was quoted as the 'Principal Sponsor'. Then came Shell (fuel and oil), Courtaulds (fibres and chemicals), Hugo Boss (clothing), Goodyear (tyres), TAG-Heuer (watches and timing), Hercules (composite material and technology), Showa (shock absorbers) and Shueisha (publishing), followed by 'Official Suppliers': Brembo (brakes), Lista (storage cabinets), SKF (bearings), Templeman (carbon fibre tooling) and Voko (office furnishings).

'The Operation' covered McLaren International, working from a 67,000 sq. ft factory and office complex based at Woking Business Park and directly employing more than 175 people. Honda's engine supply base was 35 miles away, at Langley in Berkshire, acting as a European out-station for Honda's research and development department at Wako, near Tokyo. 'The Car' would be a Marlboro McLaren Honda MP4/5B, powered by a Honda RA100E V10.

So far, so good. When it came to 'The Drivers', however, the compiler of the information sheet must have taken a deep breath when adding 'Ayrton Senna'. To all intents and purposes, the previous differences between Ayrton and the sport's governing body appeared to have been patched up after a stand-off stretching into the week leading up to the first race in the United States.

Shuttle diplomacy between Woking, Paris and Brazil by Ron Dennis had seen Senna's refusal to back down and FISA's reluctance to issue a licence dilute at the last minute to statements of mutual respect which were formal rather than effusive. That said, nothing would be certain until the necessary documentation was signed in Phoenix – assuming Ayrton turned up in the first place. Rarely can a race headquarters have been more popular with the media than on Thursday, 8 March 1990, when Senna arrived and was proffered the appropriate piece of paper for signature.

Ron Dennis *I think both Ayrton and I knew it wasn't going to be fixed in five minutes. It's about understanding. When someone has a problem in any company, one of the functions of management is to support the weaknesses of people, not to expose them to the world. If you're trying to get the best out of people, you identify their weaknesses and either assist them to come to terms with them themselves, or educate them around the weaknesses; you position them in the organisation with a support structure. In a more refined, highly tuned situation – such as the relationship between a racing driver and the management of the team – that becomes a more sensitive and delicate operation. When a driver like Ayrton is down you don't do things to make him further down; you don't question his ability to drive. You say: 'Hey come on, let's talk about it, let's have a realistic approach.' You don't say: 'Drink this glass of medicine and it'll all be better.' My motivation was a lot stronger coming back than his.*

AYRTON PLAYED THE GAME IN A PERFECT WAY. HE WAS ABLE TO UNDERSTAND DETAILS QUICKER THAN ME. HE WAS A LITTLE BIT AHEAD EVERYWHERE.
GERHARD BERGER

The second driver in the McLaren information sheet was listed as Gerhard Berger, Alain Prost having left for Ferrari after six successive seasons with McLaren. Apart from the obvious and immediate reduction of tension between McLaren's drivers, the arrival of the more laidback Austrian would have a beneficial long-term effect on Ayrton, as Gerhard introduced an element of fun away from the track. On it, however, the battle lines would be drawn as intensely as ever – with first blood to Berger.

Gerhard Berger

In my career, I faced a number of good drivers like [Michele] Alboreto, [Nigel] Mansell and [Thierry] Boutsen. I never faced anybody that worried me about speed. So I go to McLaren and I think Ayrton's just another driver; no problem. I remember the first day in Phoenix, I was quickest and I started from pole [second qualifying the next day had been wet]. So I say: 'Okay, another one, no problem.' In the race, I was ahead of Ayrton but then [after nine laps] I hit the brake pedal too hard, my foot caught the throttle and I went into the barrier. Ayrton went home to Brazil and thought about it.

Ayrton played the game in a perfect way. I began to realise he was so much more experienced than me. I had started racing very late but he had been karting and doing all these things as a kid. He was able to understand details quicker than me. He had seen them before, whereas I still was in a learning period, even though we were the same age. I could see from the telemetry that my disadvantage was not the speed; I was losing out to him because of all the things he could put together; everything, from setting up the car, the politics, concentration and physical condition. As a package, he was a little bit ahead everywhere.

But I had no reason to complain to him or to the team. I had to do my homework. I learned about discipline and the concentration capability he had; the attention to detail that made him the way he was. Of course, he had unbelievable natural speed. But then I think we all had. The difference was he could put everything together. Out of 100 per cent, he would have 98 per cent right.

*I think he enjoyed my way of life, and he took something from it. But at the end of the day, he just played a game because day and night he was thinking about how he f***s your racing. Look, I really liked him a lot. But Ayrton was extremely selfish. He'd be a bastard, all of those things, but in a sympathetic way. That's*

Gerhard Berger brought a new dimension to the team, not least for Senna after a tense two years working alongside Prost.

how it should be. You're not going to be
World Champion and win races just being
the nice guy. But people did not criticise
him. They did not realise it because he'd
been such a nice guy at the same time.
Very clever. He was the same as Michael
Schumacher in this sense, but he did it in a
much better way.

That would be demonstrated from the
outset as Senna won the race on the
streets of Phoenix and went on to claim
pole position in the next four, winning
two of them (Monaco and Canada), but
not in Brazil where he was taken out by a
backmarker while leading. Ayrton would
admit that his motivation, as Ron Dennis
suggested, had been weakened by the
shenanigans with Balestre, but events on a
revamped Interlagos track – the collision
not withstanding – had changed all that.

Ayrton Senna

*I got my motivation back there. I had
two weeks [following Phoenix] to
think about it and then I faced the
challenge of driving at home. I saw the
enthusiasm from all the people. They
gave me the pleasure, the fire to get in the
car again. It was only the people of Brazil
and the positive thoughts they had for me
which gave me the ingredients to restart
my career.*

THE PEOPLE OF
BRAZIL GAVE ME
THE PLEASURE,
THE FIRE, TO GET
IN THE CAR AGAIN.
AYRTON SENNA

More than 65,000 fans give voice as Senna leads Berger
during the opening lap at Interlagos. The Williams of
Boutsen and the Ferraris of Prost and Mansell give chase.
The Dallara of de Cesaris is already in the gravel at the
first corner.

Thoughts that his career might include a second World Championship were put in doubt when Prost headed the 1990 points table for the first time after successive wins in Mexico, France and Britain. Senna responded with victories in Germany, Belgium and Italy. But Prost was never far away thanks to being runner-up twice, the podium at Monza leading to an unexpected rapprochement between the Frenchman and his nemesis.

It hadn't seemed that way when the first three finishers filed into the media centre for the post-Italian Grand Prix interviews. Rather than sit in the middle and have Prost to one side, Senna persuaded Berger (who had finished third) to take centre stage and separate the former team-mates. It may have been a provocative move but it actually prompted a journalist to ask how much longer it would be before Prost and Senna reached some sort of accommodation after more than a year of non-communication. There was silence for a moment or two.

Alain Prost *I tried to shake hands with Ayrton at the first race of the season. Ask him.*

Ayrton Senna *I did not think he was entirely sincere about it. If I had, I would have shaken his hand. It is not easy to forget what happened between us last season. However, although we don't have many things in common, we share the same passion for Formula 1 and this is very important for us. When he is able to say he is sincere in front of everyone, I will accept it. I don't have a problem with that.*

Alain Prost *Yes, this is very important. Ayrton is right about that: he has his ideas about what happened last year and I have my ideas. Whatever happened, I would like to forget it. We do have the same passion for the sport. I believe I have changed a lot since last year and perhaps I understand some things more clearly than I did. I think it would be good for our sport if today as we go into the last four races if we could somehow go together. So if Ayrton agrees …*

Nigel Mansell may have won for Ferrari in Portugal but
Senna was content with scoring two more points than Prost
(above). The tables would be turned when Prost won the
next race in Spain and Senna retired (right).

After a brief pause, they stood up and shook hands. No one – least of all the drivers, you suspected – could quite believe it. As the media centre broke into spontaneous applause, Alain and Ayrton slapped each other on the back. Peace. For now.

Senna's championship lead extended to 18 points when he finished second in Portugal but the momentum and personal priorities would shift unexpectedly a week later at Jerez in Spain.

There were 12 minutes of first qualifying for the Spanish Grand Prix remaining when Martin Donnelly's Lotus crossed the start/finish line to begin a quick lap. As Donnelly flicked the yellow car into the first of two fast right-handers, the left-front suspension broke and sent the Lotus straight into a crash barrier mounted close to the edge of the track.

The enormity of the 160-mph impact beggared description as Donnelly was flung from the disintegrating car. He was still strapped to his seat, the violence of the collision having torn the bulkhead, to which the upper seat belt mounting points were attached, clean away from the car. Donnelly lay motionless on his side, his left leg hideously bent. It seemed he could not have possibly survived such a colossal blow.

With the crash occurring near the end of the lap, it took the medical car with Professor Sid Watkins on board over two minutes to reach the scene of destruction. Watkins

and a Spanish anaesthetist inserted suction and oxygen tubes before slowly removing Donnelly's helmet.

While the resuscitation process continued, Watkins was unaware that Senna had vacated his McLaren and gone straight to the scene. There he would witness, probably for the first time, the terrible devastation that can be wrought when a F1 car goes out of control. Ayrton was ashen-faced as he walked back to the McLaren motorhome, where he sat quietly on his own for several moments and gathered his thoughts.

Martin Donnelly

I live in Norfolk and when I first went there in the 1980s, Ayrton had just joined Lotus and he had a flat in Norwich. I knew him pretty well. When he came to the scene in Jerez, he'd been watching a man he knew who was near death, bone sticking out of one of his legs. He later told a journalist that seeing me like that made him realise how fragile we all are. Then he went back to the McLaren garage, got in the car, put the visor down and, when they ran the last eight minutes of the session, he set the fastest lap anybody had ever done round Jerez. Then he came straight to the medical centre once he got out of the car. All of that said a lot about Ayrton on many counts.

Having been stabilised, Donnelly was removed to hospital in Seville for a long and complex operation to attend to the leg fractures.

Professor Sid Watkins

The next morning, the news about Martin was good. I was waiting at the pit exit for Saturday practice to start when Senna came to see me. Leaning against the pit wall, he told me he had watched the resuscitation and in his serious style questioned me about the technicalities involved. He had noticed that the airway had gone in, apparently wrongly, upside down and then had been rotated and he wanted to know the anatomical reason for doing this. I showed him the kit and he was intrigued about the trick. He also asked why I had put my finger in Martin's mouth before getting the airway in. I told him this was to find a possible gap in his teeth – which there was.

Ironically, as Professor Watkins would later note in his memoirs, it was the same drill he would follow on Ayrton at Imola on 1 May 1994.

Meanwhile, Senna's mood of circumspection would not be helped when he retired from the race with a radiator holed by a stray underbody stay from an AGS. It was a fluke occurrence but that did not help Senna's peace of mind because he realised it would have been impossible to beat Prost's on-form Ferrari. Suddenly, Ayrton's 18-point lead had been halved. There were two races to go. The Japanese Grand Prix was next. If anywhere was likely to stoke unpleasant memories, Suzuka was the place. The uneasy peace created between Senna and Prost at Monza would literally be smashed to pieces. *Autocourse* takes up the story:

'Trouble began on race morning. At the drivers' briefing, the stewards reiterated the organisers' decision not to move pole position from the right to the left. On the Wednesday before, Senna had requested that pole be moved to the cleaner side of the track and Prost, ironically as it would turn out, had agreed with him. Senna had won pole, with Prost second quickest. The officials refused Senna's request because the grid positions had already been marked out, with pole on the right to correspond, in the traditional manner, with the first corner.

'Then it was declared that drivers would be penalised if they crossed the dotted yellow line designating the entrance to the pit lane. This Senna took as a direct reference to his incident with Prost at this very spot the year before. He became even more annoyed when the official said drivers forced to use the escape road could rejoin at the far end of it – exactly what Ayrton had been disqualified for in 1989. By the time the bumbling officials had changed their minds and decided drivers should turn around in the escape road and rejoin by facing oncoming traffic, Senna had already walked out of the briefing.

'With the threat of disqualification hanging over anyone who crossed the yellow line, it effectively ruled out the one and only overtaking spot at Suzuka. It meant, for instance, if Prost took the lead, then Senna would have to do something about it at the first corner because, quite literally, he might not get that close again. The warm-up times indicated, as everyone had suspected, that the Ferrari was a better bet than the McLaren in race trim – another reason for Senna to do everything in his power to keep ahead of Prost at the start.

'When the lights turned green, everything went exactly as Senna had predicted, Prost's Ferrari finding more grip and moving into an easy lead. By the time they reached the bottom of the hill, Prost was clear of Senna, but the Brazilian was already aiming for the inside line.

'Prost turned in. And Senna kept coming. The two cars touched, the impact wrecking Senna's left-front suspension and snapping off Prost's rear wing. They careered across the track and came to a dusty halt, deep in the run-off area. Surprisingly, no one else became involved.

I REMEMBER GETTING UP VERY EARLY IN THE MORNING TO WATCH THE FIGHT FOR THE CHAMPIONSHIP – AND IT LASTED ALL OF 10 SECONDS.
NEIL OATLEY

'Senna and Prost climbed from their cars and Alain, hoping the race would be stopped, began to run back to prepare to take the spare Ferrari. The officials, meanwhile, decided that neither car was in a dangerous position and, from the moment that declaration was made, Ayrton Senna became the 1990 World Champion.'

Mark Hannawin

Things had been pretty edgy inside the team because of this pole position business. Ron was definitely angry about what was going on and he got us to hoover the first 50 metres in front of Senna's grid slot. We had cable extensions and we were using those little Henry vacuum cleaners on wheels. We had a guy who had come from the factory to a race for the first time and he thought this was the standard thing we did before every race! Before the start, we knew something was going to happen because of the bad feeling there was, not just for Prost, but also for Balestre. We'd felt like saying to Ayrton before the start: 'Think of the lads, Ayrton. A one-two finish is worth about £450 each in bonus!' When they collided, it was no real surprise.

Neil Oatley

I only engineered Ayrton in 1990 and it was race by race. By the time the season started he was okay – perhaps Ron was dealing with the problem. He was the normal Ayrton and perhaps a little more relaxed with Gerhard in the other car. I didn't go to Japan. This was the first year F1 was on satellite; hardly anyone had it home but we had a feed at work. I remember getting up very early in the morning and going in to watch the fight for the championship – and it lasted all of 10 seconds. Gerhard then had the lead – and went off on the dirt at the start of the second lap and got bogged down. Both our cars in a heap at Turn One after two minutes!

The championship was at stake and cars were fairly even. The Ferrari was perhaps a tad quicker and, if Alain had gone into the lead, it would have been difficult for Ayrton to hang on to him. It seemed inevitable there would be a collision.

Senna, having just become 1990 World Champion, leads Prost back to the pits after their collision at the first corner in Japan (left). Ron Dennis continued to learn about his driver's utter determination to succeed once the crash helmet was on (above).

The feeling of anti-climax was immense, particularly for those who had travelled all the way to Suzuka. Initially, Senna was regarded as the guilty party by a force of about nine to one. But the mood shifted perceptibly two weeks later in Australia when Alain arrived in Adelaide unwilling to discuss the matter in a reasonable fashion and Ayrton delivered a polished performance in his defence.

Senna explained that he knew Prost had to finish in Japan, otherwise he would be out of the championship. In other words, Prost would probably err on the side of caution.

Ayrton Senna

I had that in my mind when we went to the grid. Prost made the better start, as I knew he would. I saw the gap and went for it but then I was surprised when Prost came back at me. I was surprised because it was totally unexpected for a driver of his knowledge and experience to make such a move. If I had been leading under the same circumstances, I would not have left room on the inside and if I had left room I would not, under any circumstances, have closed the door for a second time. So I think it was a major tactical mistake by him. A collision was inevitable and I did not hit him from behind, we were side by side.

There was no doubt that Prost had left the door wide open – albeit briefly. The argument was whether or not Senna was entitled to aim for a narrow gap on the assumption that Prost would avoid contact because he had to finish the race.

As the debate continued to rage in the Adelaide paddock, Ayrton gave television interviews, including one with Jackie Stewart for Australia's Channel 9. The discussion was almost terminated prematurely when Stewart asked Senna why he seemed to be involved in more accidents than the rest of the sport's champions put together.

Moving from a relaxed pose, Senna, his face flushed, sat upright and wagged his finger at the three-time World Champion. 'It is quite a mistake for you to make such a question, Stewart,' said Senna, before adding the now famous line, 'If you no longer go for a gap you are not a racing driver.'

Prost, meanwhile, did his case no good by refusing to speak to the media throughout the Australian weekend and his comments at the post-race press conference (after he had finished third) were confined to the race alone. He missed the end-of-season photograph which had taken place after the drivers' briefing and, to make matters even worse, he was also absent from the Gathering of Champions photograph that included Juan Manuel Fangio, Jack Brabham, Denny Hulme, James Hunt, Nelson Piquet, Senna and Stewart.

Above: Senna leads Mansell after lapping Alliot's Ligier in the final race in Australia.

It was noticed by this stage that Ayrton was moving around Adelaide like a man with a burden removed form his shoulders: not simply the elimination of the heavy responsibility of trying to win the Championship, but a release from the frustration of, in his words 'having the Championship taken away from me in 1989'. It was as if a score had been settled. The truth would emerge 12 months later.

Mark Hannawin

When the cars would be sitting in the garage waiting to go out for qualifying, you could see Ayrton had an amazing focus on the timing screen. He knew the exact moment to go out so that he would cross the line at the last second to do that one final lap. It would drive Gerhard mad. He would come in, see Ayrton's time and beat his hands on the steering wheel because he couldn't believe they were in the same car. Then Ayrton would start talking to his engineer on the radio and the download of information was just unbelievable. We reckoned he could count blades of grass on the inside of each corner.

There is no doubt that Senna's more relaxed state out of the car, as noted by Oatley, was indeed due to the influence and presence of Berger.

Gerhard Berger

We did some crazy things. Everyone seems to remember the story of his briefcase. Flying into Monza, I just opened the door of the helicopter and threw the briefcase out, hoping it would fall into the trees at Lesmo. But I missed it by a moment and it fell where there were some marshals, so he got it back. I couldn't believe it when I saw the guy running towards the helicopter, carrying the briefcase. Ayrton didn't think it was funny at all.

Then there's the story of going through the centre of Milan. Ayrton was driving. We were in huge traffic and people started to realise it was us. Suddenly there's hundreds of people around. The light goes green and I just reached over, took the key out and threw it out of the window. Ayrton was underneath the car – everywhere – looking for this key and people are surrounding him; dancing round him. So now there is a big, big traffic jam and the police arrive. They're going mad. Then they see it's Ayrton – and start helping him to find the key! I'll never forget seeing a big guy in a uniform, crawling around, looking everywhere on the ground for the keys. Ayrton did see the funny side of that.

AYRTON WAS CERTAINLY THE MOST FOCUSED DRIVER I EVER WORKED WITH. HE ABSOLUTELY GAVE IT HIS ALL; HE THOUGHT IT; HE SLEPT IT; HE THOUGHT ABOUT IT BETWEEN PRACTICES.
GORDON MURRAY

Ron Dennis

When Ayrton joined our team, he did not have a sense of humour. I started the process of trying to give him an understanding of the value of laughter and what a great way it was to break tension in a situation. This became an amusing mission for Gerhard and myself. Practical jokes ran consistently through the team and they were extreme. Once Ayrton realised that this had an element of competition about it, such as who could do the most outrageous thing to the other, then he very much entered into the spirit.

One of the best moments was when we were in Australia together, hatching up what we could do to really inflict pain on each other. Gerhard stole Ayrton's passport without him knowing and we surgically removed all the pictures from the passport and cut out from a very dubious magazine an equivalent size of male genitalia and carefully put it in place with Sellotape. At a glance you did not realise anything had taken place other than there wasn't a face where there was supposed to be a face. When Ayrton came back to Europe he immediately got on a plane to Brazil but, whatever the route was, he had to go through Argentina. That was the first time anyone looked at his passport. They were not amused and he spent 24 hours in Argentina because they would not allow him to pass through without his passport being rectified. But he never admitted it for months.

Viviane Lalli

Gerard and Ayrton were great friends. They would play tricks all the time on each other, like placing a frog under each other´s bed, or inside their bags at the hotel. The competition was kept for the race track; the fun for outside the track. They spent many great moments together..

Apart from the lighter moments instigated by Berger, it had been a very tough 12 months for Senna. In an interview near the end of the season, Ayrton would attribute his resilience to being a Brazilian working and living away from home.

Ayrton Senna

I believe when somebody from 10,000 km away in South America, in Brazil, decides to go to Europe, you must have in yourself a lot of guts and a lot of determination to succeed. I think that is a common feeling in all of us [from South America]. We have less knowledge around us that can do part of the job for us. We have to create much more; we have to innovate much more from our own source. We are still very young; we are still disorganised in things like language, so therefore, we have more problems when doing and achieving things. But when we decide to go for it and compete, I believe we have in our instincts a little bit more power to go through difficulties; we have the ability to imagine and create and apply this in these situations.

Ayrton gave the interview at Angra dos Reis, his beach home tucked out of sight on the coastline to the south of Rio de Janeiro. With its tennis courts and water sports, this represented Senna's favourite retreat away from the noise and hustle of motor sport. He had come a long way since the single room in a modest house in Norfolk in the early eighties to the rented detached property he shared with Brazilian driver Mauricio Gugelmin and his wife Stella in an exclusive cul-de-sac in Esher at the heart of London's stockbroker belt. Once on board with McLaren and heading towards his first championship, Senna was also on the move to Monaco and its handy location to Nice airport, not to mention the tax advantages enjoyed by several F1 drivers. But Ayrton's heart had always remained in his family's various homes in Brazil, moving on when he could to his ranch in Tatui and then,

for perfect peace and quiet, the beauty of Angra dos Reis and its forest backdrop. Here he would switch off from racing. But it would not take long to tune in again once he stepped on the plane taking him to his next race and the challenge of lapping the track faster than anyone else.

Gordon Murray was about to leave his role as technical director to mastermind the McLaren road-going supercar. He would take with him memories of a very special driver.

Gordon Murray

He was certainly the most focused driver I ever worked with. He absolutely gave it his all: he thought it; he slept it; he thought about it between practices. He often gets put down as a serious person because of that attitude but I think it was because he was just so engrossed in it and lived for it. He was so focused because, even if you don't have an engineering bent, that attitude means you get to learn everything about the car, the set-up, the engine response, the tyre choice and all the rest of it. Whereas other drivers might have turned up for practice and they'd been off skiing, or away doing something else and probably not given it much thought in between, they would arrive on the back foot. But Ayrton was absolutely not like that; he was a one hundred percenter.

If he'd been a tennis player or a football star or whatever, it would have been exactly the same thing. He just lived and breathed that and because he did, everybody took him seriously; everybody gave him respect and he got more out of the engineering staff and more out of the

tyre staff and the engine guys because of it. There's a huge difference between drivers that get to understand the engineering and get on with the team to a very, very high level, and those that can't do that. Ayrton just got so much more out of everything.

Having climbed from his McLaren in Adelaide for the last time in 1990, Senna was set to do talking of a different kind as the off-season beckoned.

6. TWO MORE CYLINDERS; ONE LAST TITLE

Having won the 1990 championship, Senna had to collect his trophy at the official prize-giving in Paris. He would put his visit to good use by spending a day with the staff at *L'Equipe*, the daily sporting bible of France. Senna made himself available for interviews, joined the journalists at lunch, had his picture taken in their offices and, later, during a boat trip with the staff on the Seine, they stage-managed the Eiffel Tower in the background of one particular shot. The following day, a full page in the newspaper was devoted to the visit. It was a PR coup extraordinaire in Prost's heartland. That done, Ayrton returned to Brazil for the off-season, leaving Berger to do the bulk of the testing.

Honda had moved from a V10 to a V12. Senna had tried the 12-cylinder for the first time the previous autumn and had not been impressed. When he returned for another test at Estoril shortly before the first race in Phoenix, he remained unconvinced – and was not slow in coming forward on the subject. 'I don't know what they [Honda] have been doing since,' he said. 'There is not enough progress and not enough power.' And with that, he left Honda to fret. Which, of course, was the prime objective of a statement delivered into the hands of grateful media.

Senna had spent $8.5 million on a British Aerospace 125, a twin-engine mid-size business jet that could, at a push, take him from Europe to Brazil non-stop. As soon as he left the unhappy test at Estoril, Ayrton and his pilot flew to London Heathrow, where he collected Professor Sid Watkins and his wife and then flew on to Edinburgh.

Professor Sid Watkins

It was Friday 21 February 1991. He stayed at our house in Coldstream in the Tweed Valley and the next day we went for lunch in a nearby hotel, where nobody recognised him – and that pleased him immensely. Ayrton had always wanted to go to the Jim Clark Museum at Duns and arrangements had been made with the curator for us to visit that afternoon. The one proviso Ayrton made was that it was to be a private visit; no press, no publicity and, apart from the staff at the museum, nobody else was to know. Next to Fangio, Jimmy was the driver Senna most admired.

I was driving as we went into Duns and, turning into the road where I thought the museum was, I hesitated, looking for a signpost to indicate its precise location. 'There's the sign to it,' said Ayrton. 'Where?' I replied. 'At the top of the road,' he said. 'It says Jim Clark Museum.' I couldn't even see the post the sign was on, never mind the inscription. Extraordinary visual acuity was one of Senna's attributes, as it is with most F1 drivers.

That evening, Senna gave a talk at Loretto, Jim Clark's old school.

WE WENT FOR LUNCH IN
A NEARBY HOTEL, WHERE
NOBODY RECOGNISED
AYRTON – AND THAT PLEASED
HIM IMMENSELY.
PROFESSOR SID WATKINS

Professor Sid Watkins

After the talk he took questions for about 20 minutes or so. He was absolutely super. After having photographs taken in the Loretto Chapel, where there is a plaque to Jimmy, we had supper in the headmaster's quarters with some of the Sixth Form and some of the older boys. The Bishop of Truro was there and he and Ayrton got into a nice little chat about religion because, of course, they were on opposite sides of the wall: Anglican and Roman Catholic. After the meal, Ayrton had to leave. I took him to the airport and he flew back to Portugal.

In an interview with the writer Christopher Hilton, the Bishop of Truro, Michael Ball, would later recall his meeting with Senna.

Michael Ball, Bishop of Truro

His personality was attractive and he had a lovely sense of humour. Obviously he had a very deep faith. I'd almost call him a born-again Catholic. He had been nurtured in his faith but somehow we all gained the impression that, at some stage in his life, it had become renewed and he had found a very deep faith. Born-again is an extreme term. But one felt that somehow or other he had recovered his faith.

In an interview the previous year with his friend and journalist, Russell Bulgin, Senna had been asked for his view on having a God-given talent.

Ayrton Senna

I think anything that you are aware about in your life, and many other things about which you are not aware, were given to you by Him.

Whether you understand, or you don't, whether you live that way or not, that's the way it is. If you get to understand a little bit only, it makes so much more sense; makes things so much more peaceful to understand the difficulties particularly and enjoy better the good moments. So I see it as a natural thing. Unfortunately, I had not experienced that before; I wish I had found it before, but it's never too late.

Michael Ball, Bishop of Truro

I found him to be a very wonderful man. The other thing that came through was his care of the less fortunate. He told a story or two of the people on his continent and their degradation; he was very moving about that.

At the dinner we got on totally. I mean by that there was no barrier of any sort. We exchanged stories as much as anything. He acknowledged me for what I was and I did the same to him. He had this amazing ability to treat you as a friend from the word go. That was the naturalness, the sheer naturalness of the man. It was enchanting, and it enchanted the young people as well.

Honda were less than enchanted when Senna arrived in Arizona for the first race and continued to express his doubts about the McLaren-Honda package. He was not alone, although team members would not express their thoughts as freely.

The worry among the race crew was that they did not know enough about the MP4/6. The test at Estoril, because of the weather and the environment, had told them next to nothing about how the McLaren might perform on the streets of Phoenix. The car was barely two weeks old and the chassis Senna would drive (MP4/6, chassis 3) was being completed for the first time in the pit garage facing onto Jefferson Street. It would not turn a wheel until Senna drove out of the pit lane to start free practice on the Friday morning. As for the man himself, he had a heavy cold and, apart from the few laps at Estoril, he had not sat in a racing car since climbing from the crashed McLaren at Adelaide four months before. All in all, the opposition saw this as their best hope in years.

In the event, Senna and McLaren-Honda would blow them away and totally destroy the best anyone had to offer. It would be a devastating show of both Senna's ability to plug himself back into the mainstream and of McLaren's capacity to cope with a new car and an unraced engine. Senna led every lap and, at the end, he collected 10 points, the new allocation for a victory, his 27th. That put him into joint second place with Jackie Stewart in the league of all-time winners.

Number 28 would follow one week later at Interlagos, his first win at home in eight attempts. Unlike the race at Phoenix, this one had been anything but easy. Ayrton led all the way but, for the first half of the race, he was pushed exceedingly hard by Nigel Mansell's Williams-Renault. Had Mansell not dropped out with a recurrence of the gearbox trouble that struck at Phoenix, he would have been perfectly placed to take advantage as Senna ran into serious difficulties in the closing laps.

Ayrton first realised there was a problem when fourth gear went missing. Then, in his words, 'the gearbox went completely crazy'. Third disappeared and came back; fifth and sixth did likewise. Then he had nothing but neutral. On the last lap, he somehow found sixth and kept it there, even though a rain shower had doused the track and the Williams of Riccardo Patrese was closing rapidly.

Senna nursed his car on slicks and Patrese went as quickly as he dared, the first of the semi-automatic gearboxes on the Williams proving unpredictable. Senna felt sure he was about to have victory snatched away yet again. But he made it by two seconds, after an hour and 38 minutes of racing. Whatever Ayrton may have previously said about the Honda, it had served him well when it mattered most. This had been a fine example of the V12's flexibility as an engine, revving to 14,500 rpm during qualifying, but managing to stutter through the tight corners at only 5,000 rpm.

Ayrton had to keep a close eye on his mirrors during the tense closing moments of his home Grand Prix.

Barely able to hoist the winner's trophy in Brazil (above), Ayrton receives the plaudits after his fourth win at Monaco (right).

On his slowing-down lap, Senna stopped to pick up a Brazilian flag but the Honda cried, 'Enough!' and stopped. Ayrton was eventually towed back to parc fermé where he had to be lifted from his car. The physical effort required to deal with the manual gearbox had taken a terrible toll and Senna was totally spent. His back and shoulders were locked in spasm, partially because the seat harness was too tight and partly through the sheer emotion of the moment. On the rostrum, he could barely lift the trophy he coveted most.

Viviane Lalli

His first victory in Brazil is the one we remember most as a family. This was a missing victory as, every time he raced in Brazil, something unexpected happened. He was a champion already, he had won many races in different countries, but never in Brazil. It was an intense emotion for him and for all Brazilian people. The fans were in ecstasy. A huge crowd gathered in front of our parents' house, where he was recovering after the race. They stayed there for hours, until Ayrton finally went to greet them. It was a wonderful moment.

Senna would visit the top step of the podium again at Imola to establish a lead of 20 points over Berger going into the fourth round of the championship at Monaco. On the evidence of the season so far, no one expected anything other than a hat-trick of wins for Ayrton on the streets of the principality. True enough, he dominated the weekend, but not before a moment of pure Senna magic in the closing minutes of qualifying.

Bit by bit, the opposition had been nibbling away at the pole time established by Senna during the first qualifying session on the Thursday. He duly appeared in the final hour and went fastest. That seemed to be that.

What we didn't know was that Senna had missed a gear during that lap. Ayrton being Ayrton, he was not satisfied. He reappeared and, with two minutes to go, crossed the line to start his final lap. It is not an exaggeration to say the entire place held its breath waiting for red and white McLaren number 1 to appear. When it did, the pace and urgency of the moment were truly staggering. The car seemed to be dancing and shimmying faster than it could possibly go. The lap time, when announced in four languages, simply confirmed it.

We had seen this before, of course. But the difference on this occasion was the reaction of the crowd in the grandstand towering over the stretch of track running from Tabac to the first swimming pool chicane. Previously, when say Prost or Jean Alesi had gone faster in their Ferraris, there had been much yelling and leaping about in the manner of greeting the winning goal at a soccer match. On this occasion, the grandstand, from one end to the other, simply stood and applauded heartily as Senna came by on his slowing-down lap. It was an enthusiastic response but it also had a feeling of controlled reverence; a sensation that is difficult to describe. It was as though the spectators appreciated that they had been lucky enough to witness something very special indeed.

The McLaren had only been in sight for three or four seconds. There had been much for the spectators to assimilate in that short time and they were left to imagine what it must have been like on the rest of the lap as Senna recorded a time half a second faster than anyone else, a margin that covered the next five cars on the grid. Few would have bet on anyone other that Senna becoming champion for a third time.

In fact, he would not win another Grand Prix for three months. Ayrton would lose no time reiterating his belief that the Honda engine was not up to scratch. Proof that the McLaren package was in danger of being outclassed came in Canada with the Williams-Renaults occupying the front row. The British-French combination would have won had Mansell not made a monumental gaffe on the last lap when, waving presumptuously to the crowd, he allowed the engine revs to drop and lost sufficient power to drive the hydraulics for the semi-automatic gearbox. Even then, McLaren had not been there to pick up the pieces, Senna and Berger having retired with electrical and electronics problems.

In Mexico two weeks later, it got much worse when Ayrton had arguably the most spectacular accident of his career. Attempting to wrest fastest time from the Williams drivers in the last few minutes of Friday qualifying, Senna decided to take Peraltada, a steeply banked right-hander, in sixth rather than the favoured fifth gear. As the rear of the McLaren became loose midway through the 180-degree turn, he realised he was running a fraction too fast and backed off, snatching fifth gear in an effort to retrieve the situation.

Too late. The car spun out of control and flipped upside down after slamming backwards into a tyre barrier. Almost before the decision had been made to red-flag the session, Senna was crawling from beneath the car. A routine check in the circuit's medical centre revealed no serious harm had been done. Surprisingly, the same could be said for the car with damage limited to the roll hoop, a radiator, cockpit bodywork and the front-left corner. However, the wound to the team's reputation would continue to fester, courtesy of their star driver.

'The Williams is now very quick indeed,' said Senna. 'It's very hard for me to keep up the rhythm. Honda are working hard to improve the engine but the Williams chassis is much better than ours. If we don't get some new equipment then we're going to have trouble on our hands during the second half of the season.'

Behind closed doors, Senna was more direct with the engine supplier. 'You are losing me the World Championship,' he is reported to have told the Japanese engineers. 'Our competitive position should not be judged by the 44 points I have scored. In reality, Gerhard's ten points are a more accurate indication of your competitive position.'

Senna's strongly articulated views summed up an engine that was overweight, excessively thirsty and not producing the expected power. Furthermore, he was urging McLaren to push development with their semi-automatic gearbox. He felt the paddle shift would have helped avoid the accident at Peralta:

Ayrton had to be just as forceful out of the cockpit when dealing with his car's perceived shortcomings.

'To shift down from sixth to fifth under those circumstances, you really need a semi-automatic, which I hadn't got, so I was trying to compensate with my own ability,' said Senna. 'It was my mistake.'

Senna made no mistakes in the race, finishing third behind the pair of Williams, a result he repeated in France. Ayrton might have gone one better at Silverstone but for a faulty fuel read-out that caused the MP4/6 to splutter to a halt on the final lap. Six points becoming three (Senna was classified fourth, one lap down) was bad enough, but he then had to endure riding back to the pits on the sidepod of Mansell's winning Williams while the

Englishman received the adulation of the capacity crowd.

If Senna was annoyed then, he would be speechless with rage when the same thing happened two weeks later at Hockenheim. It was no consolation that 'only' fourth place had been lost as opposed to second; this time there would be no points for being classified seventh. Mansell, by winning once more, had closed to within eight points of Senna's championship lead. Ayrton hardly needed to emphasise to McLaren-Honda that they needed to react to the pressure from Williams; the message had been received loud and clear at Woking and Wako.

On the Monday before the next race in Hungary, McLaren and Honda turned up at Silverstone with 5 drivers – Senna, Berger, Allan McNish, Jonathan Palmer and Stefan Johansson – and 58 personnel. During this mammoth operation, they tried many things, including two different types of semi-automatic transmission and a reactive suspension system.

One of the gearboxes (a McLaren system as opposed to a Honda-inspired gearbox) was fitted to the spare car in Hungary. But when Senna spun across a kerb on the first day of practice and damaged

the underbody, it meant there was insufficient time to do further useful running, the car being converted back to a manual gearbox for the remainder of the weekend. It showed determination to catch up – and hold Ayrton's interest. It was no coincidence, perhaps, that a dinner hosted by Renault for the British press in Hungary heard Patrick Faure, president of Renault Sport, say that no top grand prix team 'could afford to say "No" to Senna'.

Ayrton, for his part, was utterly determined to make the most of the Hungaroring, a circuit that might at least suit the McLaren

marginally better than the Williams. His performance all weekend in Hungary was nothing short of brilliant, particularly his laps during qualifying when he beat Patrese and Mansell by more than a second. It's true that Shell had come to his aid by supplying a qualifying fuel for the first time – a practice widely used by other teams. This had been one of the things Senna had been calling for and he made good use of the extra power.

Pole at the Hungaroring would be as important as at Monaco. After brutally chopping across a less-than-amused Patrese at the first corner, Senna went on to win for the first time since Monaco. Mansell and Patrese finished second and third, the Italian using his presence on the podium to express displeasure over Senna's first corner tactics.

This came at an awkward moment for Ayrton. There had already been discussion about his driving in Germany when, according to Prost, Ayrton had the Ferrari on the grass more than once when defending position, Prost even going to so far as to claim Senna had brake-tested the Frenchman at close to 200 mph.

The continuation of this feud had resulted in Senna squeezing the Ferrari into an escape road, where the unhappy Prost had stalled. Afterwards, Prost had attacked FISA's apparent refusal to reprimand Senna. 'If regulations exist,' fumed Prost, 'they must be the same for everyone. The championship is over for me now. I will do everything I can to help Williams-Renault.'

FISA reacted by warning both drivers about their behaviour – hence Ayrton's discomfort over Patrese's outburst on the podium in Hungary. This came two days after Prost and Senna had been called by FISA to the Elf motorhome, which was considered neutral ground. They were shown videos of the German incidents, after which the officials left Ayrton and Alain to discuss their differences in private. After more than an hour, they emerged to shake hands.

Outside the motorhome, the pandemonium had to be seen to be believed, as journalists and photographers smashed tables and chairs in their anxiety to cram into the small compound and discover precisely what had been going on (there had been no official notification of this 'summit'). Neither driver would talk in detail but it did seem that a genuine effort had been made to patch up their differences. Of course, sceptical members of F1 society recalled Monza the year before and the apparent rapprochement at the press conference. A month later, they had driven into each other at Suzuka. So why should this be different?

'What has happened in the past has not been pleasant for anyone,' said Senna. 'I don't think we were ready to make peace a year ago; a set of circumstances occurred that made it impossible. But now, I have to try and believe that it will work. My honest belief is that as much as he had had enough of this, Alain has had more than I have had. I am very stable, very cool, very balanced at the moment. I think Alain has more problems than I do right now, generally speaking. That, perhaps, has had some effect on us coming together; for both of us to try.'

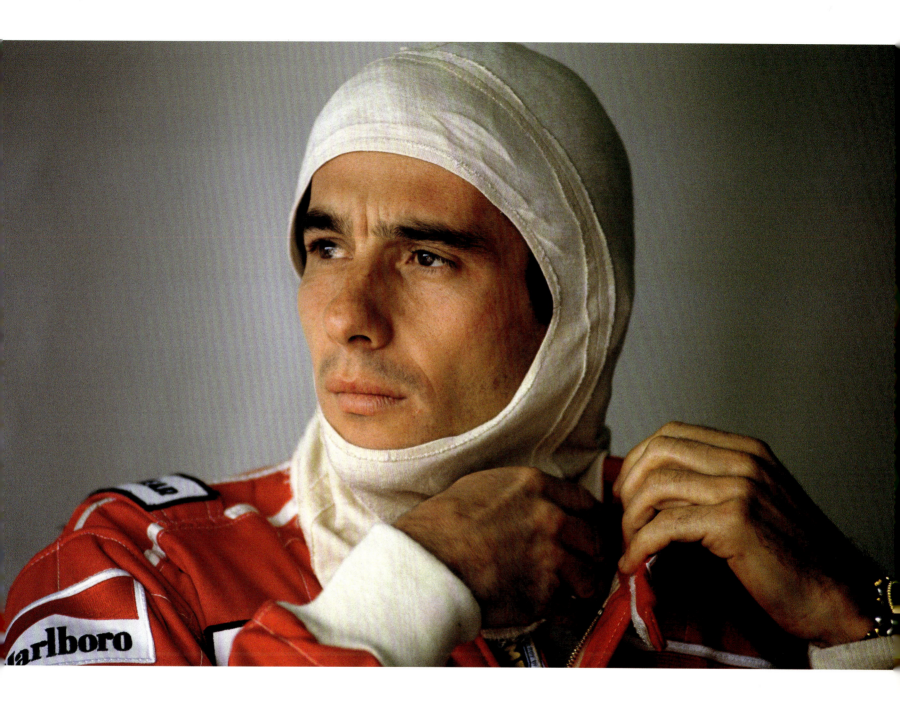

The reference to Prost's struggle to bring reform to Ferrari was true enough, but those same cynics noted that it was in Senna's interest to cease the feud, particularly with regard to Prost's earlier remarks concerning helping Williams in the Championship. Either way, both drivers seemed genuinely relieved that something positive had been done, Prost admitting he felt more relaxed during the remainder of the weekend than he had done for some time before. Which was a good thing for Alain because the Italian Grand Prix was two races away.

On the day before practice began at Monza, the McLaren engineers were called to a special meeting to discuss complaints from Senna and Berger. Despite finishing first and second at the previous race in Belgium, Ayrton and Gerhard felt they were being out-run by the Williams-Renaults (both of which had hit trouble at the Belgian Grand Prix at Spa). Views were expressed freely by all sides in the Monza meeting, and the drivers, realising that Honda were trying their hardest, apologised for their hasty remarks post-Belgium.

In the Italian Grand Prix, Senna withstood extraordinary pressure from the Williams duo until forced to give best to Mansell. Nonetheless, second place was good enough for Ayrton to maintain his lead of the championship. Mansell later commented that it had been an invigorating and fair fight. Such generous sporting camaraderie would degenerate in the final four races.

Mansell's mood went into steep decline in Portugal when he was black-flagged for the second year in succession, this time through no fault of his own. Having led the first half of the race, Mansell's championship hopes took a dive during a pit stop when a breakdown in team communications caused him to be waved back into the race before the right-rear wheel had been secured. In the heat of the moment, the wheel was re-attached while the Williams was standing in the pit acceleration lane; a clear breach of the regulations. Second place for Senna meant, with three races to go and a maximum of 30 points available, he was 24 points ahead of his dismayed and disqualified rival. But that was not to say Mansell would give up without a fight. And Ayrton knew it.

Senna locks his left-front wheel while working hard to stay ahead of Mansell at Monza.

YOU'VE GOT TO UNDERSTAND I'VE BEEN DOING THIS SINCE I WAS SIX YEARS OLD AND IT'S ALL I DO.
AYRTON SENNA

Senna had not been happy with the way Mansell had muscled into the lead from the second row in Portugal. Ayrton appeared preoccupied when he arrived in Spain a few days later, the tension being cranked up several notches in the drivers' briefing. The mood was set when Berger walked in and playfully tapped Mansell's left ankle – which happened to have been injured two nights before in a friendly football match. Mansell got to his feet and grabbed his former Ferrari team-mate; some reports saying it was a gentle shove; others claiming that he had Gerhard by the throat. Either way, there was a distinct edge in the room, not helped when Jean-Marie Balestre arrived and said the stewards would be watching certain drivers in the light of what had happened at the start in Portugal. Whereupon, Mansell was on his feet again, saying if that was the case then Balestre ought to look at some of Senna's misdemeanours in the past. Whereupon, Senna angrily retorted that Mansell had been involved in more accidents than anyone else. Happy days.

It was clear there was no love lost between the championship contenders and everyone held their breath during the race when Mansell, who had to win, drew alongside Senna on the 180 mph straight. On and on they went, both veering dangerously close; two hard men intent on out-psyching each other. In the light of what had happened in the briefing, no one dared look.

Mansell won that battle but he had to do it all again when McLaren won the pit-stop battle and Senna got out ahead of the Williams. Senna, having gone against advice and chosen hard tyres for the left of the McLaren and soft for the right, paid the price when he spun. In one of his worst races of the season, Ayrton came home an unhappy fifth. His championship lead had dropped to 16 points with two more races to run. But it would be over sooner than expected.

Seventeen minutes into the Japanese Grand Prix, Ayrton Senna became the 1991 World Champion. The acquisition of his third title was put beyond question when Mansell spun off, leaving Senna and Berger to run the race as they pleased. And they chose to go for broke. Berger, starting from pole, had rushed into the lead, a tactic that suited Senna as he kept Mansell at bay. Once Mansell had disappeared, Senna set after his

team-mate, took the lead – and then handed the race back to Gerhard within sight of the flag. All told, this was the perfect result for Honda Marlboro McLaren. They had raised their game to such an extent that Williams-Renault were blown away. For once, the race at Suzuka appeared to be without controversy. Which it was – until the post-race press conference.

Senna chose to unleash a venomous attack on Balestre, who, between Spain and Japan, had been superseded as FISA President by Max Mosley. As his pent-up emotions spilled over, Senna boldly admitted that he had deliberately pushed Prost off the road to settle the championship the previous year. It was an extraordinary monologue that clearly unburdened the Brazilian but, unfortunately, removed some of the limelight from the campaign of technical recovery carried out by his loyal team. McLaren-Honda were constructors' champions for a fourth year in succession.

Senna had won six races (he would go on to win a seventh in Australia), but Ron Dennis was concerned about the future following Ayrton's attack on the out-going president of FISA.

Max Mosley

Senna really let rip in a press conference. Ron, quite rightly, was very alarmed and concerned what Balestre, who was still president of the FIA and very powerful, would do to him by not giving Senna a licence or whatever. Ron came to me and said: 'Ayrton needs to apologise but he absolutely refuses to. Will you talk to him?'

So I invited Ayrton up to my little suite – I always got on quite well with him – and I said: 'Ayrton, there's two kinds of people in the sport. There are amateurs and professionals. The amateur does what he feels like doing; the professional does whatever will further his career. What you did about Balestre was amateur.'

He thought for a long time, and then he said: 'Yes, you're right. But what you've got to understand is that I've been doing this since I was six years old and it's all I do.' And his eyes started to well up. He was so emotional. We cobbled together a weasel statement that was put out. It wasn't really an apology but it was close. And that was the end of it.

As reigning World Champion, Senna was in demand as the off-season rolled into 1992. With typical savvy, he used the various social occasions to mend any damage to his reputation caused by events in the media centre at Suzuka on 20 October 1991.

He travelled to Paris to receive his World Championship trophy. In what he described as an impromptu gesture, Ayrton gave his crash helmet to Jean-Marie Balestre, a move on the FIA president's home territory that did much to calm their often-stormy relationship.

Some critics were not impressed. Eoin Young, a founding director of McLaren Racing in the days when he was Bruce's right-hand man, celebrated his 25th year writing a widely read weekly column for *Autocar* magazine by questioning Senna's motives. 'I'm sure,' wrote the New Zealander, 'Senna had been waiting months, years maybe, to deliver the salvo [in Japan] and he fired every "F" word with some relish and devastating accuracy. What came afterwards [the giving of the helmet] was merely modern racing politics, nothing to do with contrition.'

Maybe so, but Ayrton then set about wooing the British two days later. He flew to London for the *Autosport* Awards, the gala occasion celebrating its tenth year as arguably the social event of the season. The British weekly magazine invited more than 600 guests to the formal dinner at the Grosvenor House Hotel on Park Lane. Senna was voted International Racing Driver of the Year. After receiving his trophy and answering questions posed by Murray Walker, Ayrton used the opportunity to make a moving speech (without notes but, clearly, carefully planned) in which he paid tribute to the part British motor sport and its people had played in his career.

Those present in the room and unfamiliar with some of Senna's ways in the F1 paddock must have thought the media an irresponsible bunch to have spoken and written so critically of such a lovely man. It was a masterstroke. Unfortunately, the brilliant execution tended to undermine his excuse, proffered after the 'bad language' press conference in Japan, that he did not understand the full force of the words used because English was not his native tongue. As Young noted dryly: 'All I can say is that Senna speaks better English than a few of the British drivers I know.'

Senna rounded off the evening in London by staying until a late hour, chatting and signing autographs. Apart from Johnny

Ayrton adds his thoughts when discussing the fine detail of how to get onto the front row of the grid at Kyalami in South Africa.

Herbert, Michele Alboreto and Mark Blundell, no other Grand Prix driver was present. Which, as Young also noted, was perhaps just as well 'because they would not have stood a chance in the face of such a commanding performance by the World Champion'.

Whether or not Senna would retain the title was very much in doubt as the season previews were written. The clever money was on Williams improving their promising FW14 with a B version incorporating active ride suspension. McLaren, meanwhile, would start 1992 with a slightly modified MP4/6 while waiting delivery of the all-new MP4/7, schemed originally for round four in Spain. Events at the first two races in South Africa and Mexico would cause that plan to be accelerated, McLaren somehow shaving a month of the development time in order to have the MP4/7 ready in time for Ayrton's home Grand Prix.

Nigel Mansell had won the first two races going away, dominating all but one practice session and leading every racing mile at Kyalami and the Autódromo Hermanos Rodríguez. Senna had finished third in South Africa but retirement with transmission trouble after 11 laps finished off a troubled weekend in Mexico.

When Senna and Gerhard Berger qualified fifth and sixth, respectively, in Mexico City, it was the first time since October 1987 that a McLaren had been absent from the front two rows of the grid. It was a statistic that underlined the team's remarkable

consistency while, at the same time, illustrating an increasingly desperate bout of uncompetitiveness. Not only were Williams rubbing salt in the wound, Benetton-Ford, with the novice Michael Schumacher onboard, were getting in on the act as well.

The handling of the MP4/6, never a strong point, had been cruelly exposed in Mexico when one of the many severe bumps on the 2.7-mile track caught out Senna as he explored the limits during first qualifying. When the car broke away and slammed sideways into the barrier, Ayrton thought

he had broken both his legs, such was the
violence of the impact as a lower wishbone
speared its way through the monocoque.
In fact, only the left leg was badly bruised
around the calf muscle but it was bad
enough to have Senna undergo several
hours of physiotherapy that night. It was
21 March 1992. It was no way to spend his
32nd birthday.

The timing of the accident was unfortunate
in more ways than one. Not long before,
Ayrton had been giving his first impressions
of the new McLaren following a test
session at Silverstone. The MP4/7 broke

new ground by incorporating a fly-by-wire throttle. Coupled with the long-awaited semi-automatic gearbox, this would help to synchronise engine and gearbox speeds.

Senna made the point that such complex electronics threatened to diminish the control exercised by the driver as he became a servant of the foolproof system. In Senna's opinion, there was a danger that a driver's superior skill would no longer be able to eke out an advantage. Then he went and proved the reverse of the theory by making a tiny error of judgement, one that did not deserve such painful consequences. In some ways, retirement so soon into the 69-lap race probably came as a physical relief. He would have two weeks to rest before Brazil. The team, meanwhile, would be working their white socks off.

For the first time for many years, there were empty seats in the grandstands lining the back straight at Interlagos. A hefty hike in admission prices was partly to blame. But word was also out about McLaren's difficult start to the season. At one stage on Friday morning, it was tempting to suggest there were more McLaren personnel than spectators.

A decision to bring three new cars (MP4/7) and three MP4/6Bs meant a logistical headache of the kind that few teams other than this one could contemplate. McLaren brought 45 engineers, technicians and mechanics; Honda had 23 personnel, there were two from TAG Electronics, five from Kenwood (handling radio communications), four catering staff and, of course, Senna and Berger.

An indication of the seriousness and extent of the operation could be gauged by Dennis leaving his post at the pit wall, hovering anxiously in the garage and, when necessary, using his past experience to give the mechanics a hand. The third new chassis did not arrive until the day before practice began. Such had been the hurry to complete the build programme, the car did not have the McLaren name on its nose – thus technically breaking the rules since each car had to carry the manufacturer's name, no matter how small the lettering. No one protested because they either didn't notice or didn't care, such was the desire to have McLaren raise their game and break what looked like being a Williams stranglehold. It would be easier said than done.

During practice on Saturday, Senna's engine blew up and Berger's car caught fire. The precise cause was difficult to ascertain since the damage to the ancillary equipment was quite severe and caught out the team with regard to having sufficient spares on hand. At one stage, all six cars were in use, Berger setting some sort of record by actually driving four different cars after the engine failed on his back-up MP4/7, which had been tailored to suit Senna. It was a nightmare for the team, led by crew chief Dave Ryan.

Dave Ryan *We reached a point during practice when all six cars were either stopped out on the circuit or in some sort of trouble. I remember Ayrton being so peed off, he just drove his car in front of the garage – and floored the throttle! The Honda engines weren't good at that stage; they had been fantastic, but they lost the plot a little in 1992.*

Race day was not much better. Having swapped cars twice even before moving onto the grid, Berger found that his MP4/7 would not select a gear as the field was waved off to complete the parade lap.

Forced to start from the pit lane, Gerhard stalled, got going, only to retire with overheating. Senna held third place before the engine began to cut out occasionally. After being overtaken by three cars as he continued to suffer the misfire, Senna pulled into the pits, climbed from the car, spoke to no one, strode to his helicopter and flew home. The exhausted McLaren crew were noticeably tight-lipped when the subject of Senna's mood was raised.

Meanwhile, Mansell, behind the wheel of the dominant Williams-Renault, won again, repeating the feat in Spain and again in the San Marino Grand Prix at Imola, making it the first time a driver had won the opening five races in succession. Senna had finished third in Imola but did not make the podium. The effort required to drive an MP4/7 with trimmed wings (to make up for the Honda V12's power deficiency) had caused him to spin a couple of times in Spain and drive on the ragged edge for an hour and a half at Imola. After crossing the line, he remained slumped in the cockpit for 20 minutes.

I had some sort of cramp in my shoulders, perhaps caused by the vibration through the car and the tension involved in keeping it on the road. The shoulder straps compressed the nerves and I was being pushed against them every time the car jumped. The heat wasn't a critical factor, but it didn't help.

Meanwhile, on the podium, a delighted Mansell held up his hand to indicate the number of victories so far. There were few watching who did not believe he would require both hands to indicate the story after the next race in Monaco. But that would not account for a typically relentless and opportunist performance by Senna.

Ayrton did everything expected of him by qualifying third, a couple of tenths shy of the battling Williams duo at the front. But any thought that Mansell and Patrese would have this race to themselves would be disabused within seconds of the start.

Senna leads Mansell on the cooling down lap before spraying champagne (overleaf) in front of the Royal Box at Monaco.

Ayrton Senna *Monaco is the hardest place in the world for overtaking. I went for it at the last moment going into the first corner [Ste Devote] so as not to give Riccardo [starting from second] any indication, because otherwise he would have closed the door, of course. I got into second place that way but the problem was to stop the car before Mansell turned in because I was coming so quickly that I thought he might not have seen me. But it worked out okay*

and it was a good manoeuvre; the only chance I had to make a place. If Patrese had been ahead of me out of the corner, I doubt I would ever have got past him.

It was to be a hugely advantageous move in the long term, even if it was not evident as Mansell eased ahead by a second a lap.

Ayrton Senna *I knew there was no way I could beat him. It was impossible with the superiority of his car. But you never know what can happen at Monaco. So what I tried to do was go hard enough to be in a position to benefit if anything happened to Mansell. Already in the early race, I was planning for the late race.*

MONACO IS THE
HARDEST PLACE IN
THE WORLD FOR
OVERTAKING.
AYRTON SENNA

That moment came on lap 71. Coming through the tunnel, Mansell had a sideways moment, the drama of which seemed to increase each time he spoke about it after the race. Believing he had a puncture, Nigel radioed the pits. With only seven laps to go, his crew was caught unawares since the packing up process had begun – a necessity at Monaco two decades ago because of the open pits and the swarming crowd due to descend on them minutes after the race had finished.

The Williams roared in, new tyres put in place but, according to Mansell, the stop was tardy and the tyres not heated properly. McLaren, meanwhile, had urgently advised Ayrton about his rival's difficulties. A few moments later, something other than a Williams-Renault led a Grand Prix for the first time in 1992.

Now the chase began. Mansell immediately slashed the lap record, the lead diminishing from 5.1 seconds to 4.3 to 1.9 seconds in successive laps. There were three remaining.

IN QUALIFYING, AYRTON WOULD ALWAYS TIGHTEN HIS BELTS SOME MORE. HE WAS EITHER GOING TO BE ON THE FRONT ROW... OR WALKING BACK.
TYLER ALEXANDER

Senna was tired; his tyres were finished. Mansell was also tired but his car, the fastest on the track, had the benefit of fresh Goodyears. Had this been anywhere other than Monaco, it would have been job done for Mansell in a matter of minutes. But the tight confines of the streets gave Ayrton an ace card that he played with consummate ease.

Despite Mansell's theatrical lunges and brake-locking moments, Senna made the McLaren just wide enough to deny the Williams an opportunity to get alongside. Senna was wise to the limited number of overtaking places and Mansell, lacking the craftiness of his rival, telegraphed each attempt with the subtlety of a bull in a china shop. On this day, on this track, Mansell was never going to get by.

For Senna, this was victory number five at Monaco, for which he earned the Graham Hill Trophy in recognition of his feat in matching the Englishman's record at Monte Carlo. Mansell may have been 38 points ahead of Senna in the championship but the thing that bothered him most was criticism of his rather crude attempts to overtake. More interesting for McLaren was Mansell's claim that the Honda's acceleration out of Portier was superior to the Renault and denied Nigel the opportunity to get close enough under braking for the favoured spot into the harbour chicane.

The Englishman's continuing displeasure with life in general was not helped when Senna was fastest during first qualifying at the next race in Montreal. His mood was palpably thunderous the following day when track conditions were slower. Even though the Williams was clearly the fastest car on the track, all Mansell had to show for his work was third on the grid. He had won pole in the previous six races; now he wasn't even on the front row.

Senna, on pole for the first time since Australia the previous year, described the McLaren-Honda as being like a rocket out of the tight corners but he was less complimentary about the handling through anything resembling a quick corner. Mansell had seen that for himself and knew if he were to win this race, he would need to get ahead of Senna as soon as possible.

Mansell quickly dealt with team-mate Patrese (starting from the front row) but did not quite manage to snatch the lead from Senna. For the first 14 laps, the leading bunch ran nose to tail. It was clear that Ayrton was holding everyone up but there was little anyone could do on a track that was bumpy and dirty off-line. Undaunted, Mansell switched off the rev-limiter and launched a late attack as the leaders screamed down the straight towards the final chicane.

Ayrton saw him coming and left the minimum amount of room on the inside. Late braking off-line at close to 190 mph was never on and Mansell, realising he was not going to make it, appeared to have a go at straight-lining the chicane. The kerb did its work and destroyed the nose wings and underbody, Mansell then appearing in front of Senna at the exit, where he spun to a halt in full view of the pit wall. He remained in the car for a whole lap. (No one could be sure why he did that. Getting the race stopped would have been pointless since the use of spare cars would not have been permitted.) Once on his feet, Nigel marched to the McLaren pit and raged at Ron Dennis. Then he went to see the FISA officials and rage at them. To no avail.

Gerhard Berger *I was fourth, just behind Patrese, and saw what happened. I'd been thinking about getting past Riccardo but it was too risky; the track was just too bumpy and dirty. Nigel took a big risk and it was unnecessary that early in the race. He got off-line, didn't have enough grip and didn't make the corner. Ayrton kinda invited him in with just enough room, but no more. You could see this accident coming. I'm sure Ayrton must have been smiling when the Williams went straight on with bits of bodywork everywhere!*

The following morning's *Montreal Gazette* carried a picture of the Williams bouncing off the kerb, bodywork flying in all directions. The headline read: 'Going to Pieces'. It was an apposite summary. The race report detailed that Berger had won after Senna had been forced to retire with electrical trouble. It had almost been a double-whammy for McLaren at post-race scrutineering when Berger's rear wing was initially found to be fractionally too wide due to the protruding heads of screws securing a flap.

Senna would win two more races in 1992 but the impact of both would be diluted by alternative newsworthy events. The win in Hungary coincided with Mansell clinching the championship at an early stage to underline the superiority of his car. Senna's win at Monza a month later on 13 September 1992 will be remembered more for the paddock being convulsed with rumours and extraordinary stories. In the space of one weekend, it was confirmed that Honda would be pulling out of F1, Mansell was quitting (ultimately to race Indycars), and Senna's future remained unclear after a couple of months talking to other teams, most notably Williams.

Ayrton enjoyed nothing more than winning and waving the national flag for his adoring Brazilian fans.

Senna's disquiet was aggravated by Prost, of all people, returning to F1 after a year's sabbatical to drive the Williams, a car which had to be a shoo-in for the 1993 championship. The McLaren, on recent performances, seemed unlikely to do the job.

Neil Oatley

The move from the V10 to the V12 in 1991 hadn't been a big power step; it was heavy, more ungainly and a bit longer. In retrospect, Honda would have been better evolving the V10. It was well into the season before the power of the V12 went ahead of where we had been before. The same thing had happened in 1992 with the second V12 engine. It wasn't until after Montreal that we got ahead of where we had been the previous season. In effect, we wasted effort in those projects that would have been better served elsewhere.

Dave Ryan

It was getting very tense between Ayrton and Ron. I remember giving Ayrton a lift from Silverstone after a test to one of the little airports somewhere. Ayrton opened up about how Ron wasn't being fair. Ayrton felt very aggrieved about what was going on and the way things were happening. I don't know what had gone on.

If Senna was to leave, he would be missed by many of those working at McLaren, none more so than Tyler Alexander, with the team since the start, first as a mechanic before becoming one of the most respected crew chiefs in motor sport. The straight-talking American knew a top driver when he saw one.

Tyler Alexander

Having worked with Ayrton for several years, the first thing you would have to say is that he was just damn good! He had a lot of passion for what he did and an ability to stay focused on what he needed to do, even when there was chaos around him. He helped me on numerous occasions when I was having some issues getting something done – which I'd like to think meant the respect went both ways. His ability to get the most out of the car, and himself, always more than just amazed us. Keith Barnard, one of the mechanics who worked on Ayrton's car, did up the seat belts as tight as he could. In qualifying, when Ayrton would always tighten them up some more, Keith thought he was either going to be on the front row – or walking back. There was one occasion, during a lull in testing at Estoril, when we happened to start chatting. It was interesting because I discovered Ayrton knew a lot of stuff about the team that he'd never mentioned to me in the time that he and I worked together. He asked a whole bunch of questions, wanted to know what I thought about this and that. We were there for an hour and a half or something; just sitting on the ground out the back of the garage. He really had a good grasp of everything that was going on around him. Someone once wrote: 'In order to do anything in the world worth doing, we must not stand shivering on the bank and thinking of the cold and danger – but jump in and scramble through as well as we can.' Ayrton did that.

Unsure of his future in F1, never mind with McLaren, Senna took himself off in December to test-drive the Penske Indycar at Firebird Raceway in Phoenix. He had a lot to think about when he got back to Brazil for his usual off-season break.

Bianca Lalli

He was obviously thinking a lot about his future but I never got the impression he was going to give up F1. He was negotiating and, on this occasion, I think he was quite upset because certain parts of the contract were not as agreed and then he got a bit pissed off. It was like after Japan in 1989: he was very straight and expected other people to be the same. But we always thought he would be staying in F1. And probably with McLaren. It was difficult to imagine him being anywhere else.

AYRTON FELT VERY AGGRIEVED ABOUT WHAT WAS GOING ON AND THE WAY THINGS WERE HAPPENING.
DAVE RYAN

8. THE LONG GOODBYE

Ayrton Senna weighed in at 73 kg. The revelation was not that he was of average weight compared to the other 26 drivers, or that he tipped the official F1 scales 10 kg heavier than Alain Prost. The surprise was that he was there at all.

When the South African Grand Prix was postponed from 28 February to 14 March 1993, it merely seemed to prolong the agony of a drawn-out and tense off-season. In the midst of uncertainty about whether or not Williams would be racing (thanks to the accidental late submission of their entry form), there was endless speculation over who would drive for McLaren.

Senna had muddied the waters with his Indycar test in December 1992 and then disappeared, as usual, to Brazil to consider his options. A sixth season with McLaren did not seem to be one of them in the light of the team's failure to secure engines from Renault and what appeared to be the compromise of a customer deal with Cosworth, already in a strong relationship with their favoured partners, Benetton-Ford. But that did not account for McLaren producing MP4/8, a demon little car to accommodate the neat Ford HB V8.

Under the direction of Neil Oatley and a design/engineering team including Tim Goss (to become technical director in 2013), McLaren International began an intensive and independent development programme with an associate company, TAG Electronics Systems, to rush through a car not finalised until the last minute due to the late deal with Cosworth. The plan was to make the most of an engine more compact and fuel efficient than the Honda V12 had ever been. This would be done in tandem with further refinement of the computer-controlled active suspension, electronic engine management, chassis control, data acquisition and telemetry systems, supplemented by a lightweight electronic cockpit management system. This may be old hat today but, in 1993, it was state of the art.

MP4/8 was finally unveiled on 15 February 1993, a month before the first race at Kyalami. Even then, no one was sure if Senna would race it. There had been discussions in the Philip Morris headquarters in Lausanne, Ayrton and Ron Dennis sitting round a table with Marlboro's John Hogan and Julian Jakobi, Senna's manager.

John Hogan

We wheeled and dealed all day. Ayrton may have been bluffing about not racing if no deal was done. But who was going to take the risk?

A compromise was reached. We assumed if we all worked together, we could persuade other sponsors to up the ante, including Shell as well as ourselves. It was agreed that he would work on a race-by-race basis in negotiation with Ron.

Gerhard Berger had gone back to Ferrari and, in his place, McLaren had signed Michael Andretti. The 1991 Indycar Champion had been able to test an MP4/7 with the Honda V12 at the end of 1992 but then had to twiddle his thumbs while waiting for the new car to arrive. And when MP4/8 did finally appear, the team could not be blamed for focussing on Senna when he flew from Brazil to the chilly expanses of Silverstone.

It would be worth the trip. Ayrton was immediately impressed with MP4/8. But no one outside McLaren – and most of those within the team – knew if Senna would race in South Africa. When he did arrive, the detail of his arrangement was not made clear during a press conference at the track.

In a room with a low and grubby translucent roof, Mika Hakkinen (signed as test driver), Senna, Dennis and Andretti sat at a table in front of a temporary backdrop with Marlboro, McLaren and Shell insignia hastily arranged along the top. By today's immaculate standards, such a place would be deemed completely unacceptable. But, in 1993, the priority was to put across a message that all was well within McLaren International.

'It's the team's intention that all three Marlboro McLaren drivers will race this year,' said Dennis. 'How do we intend to cope with three drivers? As you know, there are now only 26 cars in the World Championship. There is a strong possibility that if that number drops below 25, we will in fact field a third car. It would not be at all Grands Prix. It would be at some. There are other situations that could develop. We have a very strategic approach to this year's World Championship, and this has led to a very unusual situation having developed between Ayrton and the team. Over the last few years, Ayrton and I have banged heads over a whole range of issues. We have tried to put those periods behind us.

'I think we surprised a few people at Silverstone [last week] with our performance. It is obviously a credit to the drivers but also, I think, to our engineers, who have done a very good job during the winter. Michael has been struggling with the Honda-powered MP4/7. I suppose he should be grateful that he didn't have to race it at all through last year. He is obviously a lot happier with what he has got now. And of course on my extreme right is Mika. I consider Mika to be on the ascension as a grand prix driver. It is particularly painful for him not to be racing here, but I hope the pain won't continue for too long. I have made a commitment to him, to all the drivers, to give him the best the team can.'

In the absence of detail over the arrangement with Senna, it was not difficult to guess the thrust of the first question from the floor regarding a contract – if any. 'Yes, we do have a contract with Ayrton at the moment,' said Dennis. 'As I said earlier, the contractual issues are of secondary importance. I think if you asked Ayrton if he was going to drive in Brazil [the second race of the season] that might answer your question.'

After Dennis had replied to questions about the new car, Senna took the microphone.

'Once I tried the car, I believed it has tremendous potential,' said Senna. 'I don't know – and no one on the team can know – what is the full potential of this car. It looks like it can go really fast, around one lap. We don't know about reliability; it's too early and the mileage has not been enough, and we don't know about its consistency over a race distance. We don't know how it will perform on different types of circuit because it is all-new. Normally, when you drive a racing car for the first time, your instincts will tell whether it is good or not. Of course, this is providing you have got some experience and some reference on which to base your judgement, but it is your instincts that will tell you whether the car is good, half-good – or real trouble. I may be proved wrong – I hope not – just the same way I thought last year's was not a great car when I first tested it. I thought I could be proved wrong and unfortunately I wasn't wrong. So, I hope this time again the feeling is correct because I know that the potential is there. It is only a question of time and being able to develop it properly.'

No mention had been made of money. Despite Dennis's reference to the next race in Brazil, there seemed no doubt that Senna's appearance would be for this race only, subject to on-going agreements. Whatever the detail, Ayrton was about to prove precisely why F1 in general and McLaren in particular needed his presence on the grid.

Hammering it home. Ayrton brought Interlagos to its feet
as he pushed the McLaren MP4/8 to its limits and received
the champagne at the end of 71 laps.

The South African weekend boiled down to a battle between Senna and his nemesis. Prost eventually won pole but there was no doubt that had Ayrton not been present, Alain would not have needed to raise his game to such a high level with the excellent Williams-Renault FW15.

It would be the same in the race as the two fastest men in F1 engaged in a magnificent duel. This being Prost's first race for more than a year, his total commitment was impressive as he rushed side by side with Senna through the sweeping curves behind the pits. Prost may have won the race, Senna having had problems from early on with the active suspension, but both drivers had proved a point to their respective teams. McLaren as a team were more confident than at any point during the previous troubled three months. But even allowing for Senna's ability, few of the men and women in red and white would have predicted the outcome of the next two races. Had you said rain would play a part in both, however, the odds on a Senna win would have shortened massively.

Brazil started in the dry, the Williams pair of Prost and Damon Hill looking to be in control until the skittish weather, so typical of Interlagos, doused the main straight but left the lower section just about manageable on slicks. Despite being black-flagged for overtaking under a yellow flag (a penalty that infuriated Senna and, if anything, sharpened his resolve even further at home), McLaren number 8 moved into second place at half-distance, his situation having being improved by Prost aquaplaning off the track. Hill, in only his second race as a Williams driver, was easy meat as Senna slithered into a lead he would not lose. His nephew, Bruno, later to become a F1 driver, was attending his first Grand Prix.

ORLD
MPIONSHIP
DO BRASIL
TICA
SABOR.
Canon
CAMEL
elf
Marlboro
McLAREN INTERNATIONAL
NACIONAL
Shell

Bruno Senna

It would turn out Brazil 1993 and 1994 would be the only opportunities I would ever get to see Ayrton at a race track. I went to the practice sessions in '93 and then watched the race from home. I remember him coming back afterwards and it was crazy; absolutely crazy. It was just like after the '91 race, when he came back to his parents' house in São Paulo. We had a great family celebration and there was, I'm not joking, thousands of people in front of the gate, celebrating. It was madness!

Ayrton later returned to the team and partied long into the night, his uncharacteristic exuberance bringing on a sore throat and the need for antibiotics the following day. His personal discomfort would have been soothed further by the points tables showing Ayrton and his team to be leading their respective championships. And Senna had not yet finished weaving his magic. Discussion about his future was about to be put on hold during a mesmerising few laps of Donington Park on 11 April.

When a race, scheduled for a new circuit in Japan, was cancelled at short notice, Tom Wheatcroft grabbed his chance. Donington Park was one of millionaire Wheatcroft's many assets; staging a Grand Prix there a long-held dream of the bluff and jovial builder. Apart from a last-minute rush to have the track raised to the required standard, the other drawback was that the race, to be known as the European Grand Prix, would be held over the Easter weekend; a good thing if the weather was kind but bad news if the holiday forecast followed its traditional unpleasant pattern.

Sure enough, the conditions were miserable on the first day and the last. In between, as the sun beat down on the Saturday, Senna lost the advantage that had given him fastest time in the wet on Friday and he qualified fourth behind the Renaults and Michael Schumacher's Benetton. Rain on race day would be his only hope.

It came in fits and starts, with no clear indication of what to expect once the race got under way at 2 p.m., the only certainty being the need for rain tyres at the green light. The first few moments were not brilliant for Senna as he was squeezed by Schumacher, a move that allowed Karl Wendlinger into fourth. The Sauber driver's stay in that position would be brief. Truly fired up, Senna was about to produce a first lap performance of astonishing quality and opportunism.

He quickly overtook Schumacher, ran round the outside of Wendlinger on the downhill Craner Curves, appeared through the spray to take Hill on the climb to McLeans and then outbraked Prost into the Melbourne Hairpin as if the Williams were standing still. In just over 80 seconds, Senna had gone from fifth to first. His lap had taken 1 minute 35.843 seconds. Prost had completed the lap in 1 minute 36.541 seconds; Hill, 1 minute 36.963 seconds. And so it went on. Lap two: Senna, 1 minute 27.882 seconds; Prost, 1 minute 31.429 seconds. Lap three: Senna, 1 minute 28.203 seconds; Prost, 1 minute 30.722 seconds. An extraordinary display by any standard. The problem now was tyre choice as the rain would come and go with such varying degrees of intensity that teams and drivers had to call their tactics by the lap.

Apart from a brief reshuffle during one sequence of pit stops, car number 8 remained in the lead for the hour and 50 minutes it took to run this race. Senna did not put a foot wrong and the embattled squad of mechanics did an excellent job as pit calls usually matched the changing conditions. When they didn't, Senna's deft touch would make the difference.

Dave Ryan *I was running Andretti. It was the only time we'd ever have a Grand Prix at Donington and everything about the place was Mickey Mouse. We had a hydraulic problem on the spare car and I remember working on it on race morning under a tarpaulin in front of the garage.*

There were loads of pit stops in the race and Ayrton got the fastest lap thanks to driving right through the pits at one point because we were dealing with Andretti at the time. Ayrton was unbelievable: he was just on fire that day.

Senna won by more than a minute and came close to lapping the rest of the field, led by Hill and Prost. If the mood within McLaren was ecstatic, it was less so at Williams where Prost and his team disagreed over tactics that had usually seen the Frenchman on the wrong tyres at the wrong time.

Mesmerising at Donington. Having dispensed with Karl Wendlinger's Sauber on the Craner Curves, Ayrton lines up the Williams pair, Damon Hill (0) and Alain Prost (2) prior to taking the lead at the end of the first lap. Twelve months later, Senna and Hill would be team-mates.

There was no doubt Ayrton enjoyed Alain's discomfort at the post-race press conference as Prost mumbled about his car and explained a stalled engine at one of the many pit stops by saying the clutch on the Williams was very difficult. At which point, Senna leaned across and offered to swap cars. He was in a happy frame of mind.

Ayrton Senna

I don't know how many times we stopped for tyres. I think it's surely the record in any race. Driving with slicks in the damp and very slippery conditions was a tremendous effort because you just don't get the feeling from the car. You have to commit yourself to certain corners and you can be off the circuit. Conditions like this is gambling and taking chances that pay off and we gambled well. I feel very light about it all. I wish I could go home and have another party like Brazil. Then I would have another week of bad throat and antibiotics but I would go through it again. We won as a group. So many things happened that I find it hard to remember.

The race told me everything about myself; it was what I wanted to prove to myself. A natural tendency for a driver, as long as he is able to do his job with a team, is to learn continuously. Experience only adds to your driving, providing you can keep your motivation at a single level. I think that's been the case almost every year of my career from 1984, always just a little bit better – not necessarily faster, but more consistent; less susceptible to mistakes, thinking always, always, always. That experience allows you to be a step ahead all the time, ready to make the next move in a race.

That doctrine could also have been applied to life outside the cockpit, judging by what he did next. Ayrton rubbed further salt into Prost's wound by closing his eyes and putting his head back feigning sleep during one of Prost's answers. Perhaps that was when Senna worked out how he could further use the occasion to his advantage.

When asked about his car, Senna proceeded to lambast Ford for not giving McLaren the same specification V8 as that supplied on an exclusive basis to Benetton. It was the perfect time to say this since McLaren had scored two wins and the best Benetton could offer was third place for Schumacher in Brazil. Compared to McLaren on 26 points in the Constructors' Championship, Benetton had a meagre six.

It was mischief-making of the highest order. Senna knew the Benetton contract was in place long before Ford's deal with McLaren had been done. Had Donington been dry, Senna also knew that Schumacher would have been in the mix, giving him a hard time. Which perhaps prompted Ayrton to go straight back to Brazil and stay there, threatening not to show up for the San Marino Grand Prix a fortnight later. After much discussion with Dennis, Ayrton arrived in the Imola paddock five minutes after practice had started. And so it would continue through the season, one negotiation leading to the next race. Then another. And another.

Indy Lall

We were at a Silverstone test – this was before emails and all of that – and Ron called to say he was sending a fax that needed to get to Ayrton. I knew it had to be a contract. I got the fax number from the circuit manager and said to him: 'There's quite a hefty document coming through from Ron and I need privacy.' When it came through, I didn't look at it. I got an A4 envelope and the sheets went straight in, one after the other. I really wanted to help Ayrton as my friend, but this was not in my league.

I gave the envelope to Ayrton and, when there was a lull in proceedings, he went to the back of the truck. He wanted to tell me what it was about. I said: 'Look, you don't have to. All I ask is just do what's right for you. But remember that what is right for you now doesn't necessarily mean it's going to be right in a year or two years' time. If you can look that far ahead, it may be tough now but it might be the right thing for later on.' From his expression, I got the impression he couldn't look that far ahead because he talked himself into the corner. So, for the remainder of the year was he was on a race-by-race basis.

Tim Murnane, McLaren's lawyer

It was every other week, usually a Tuesday or a Wednesday night, and I remember being in the office with Ron until the early hours of the next morning. Ayrton would be leveraging his position to the absolute max, almost to the point where he would say: 'I'm not getting on the plane until this is done' and then demanding certain things. Obviously, we wanted certain things as well and would drive an equally hard bargain. This was between each race and stopped after about six races, certainly well into the European part of the season. Of course, this wasn't the electronic age, so we were doing it all by fax, which meant the drama of the thing chugging through: 'Is it the right way up? Has he signed it?' All of that. That was definitely one of the more interesting things I've been involved with over the years.

I KNEW IT HAD TO BE A CONTRACT. I GOT AN A4 ENVELOPE AND THE SHEETS WENT STRAIGHT IN, ONE AFTER THE OTHER AND I GAVE IT TO AYRTON.
INDY LALL

Even though McLaren desperately wanted Senna for the sixth round at Monaco above all else, Ayrton did not expect to win it, despite his speed and experience at this unique track. The McLaren MP4/8 was unable to cope with the bumps, Ayrton having provided graphic evidence of that during the first day of practice when the McLaren suddenly snatched to the left on the approach to Ste Devote, hit the barrier and then cannoned into the Armco on the opposite of the track. All four corners were wiped off the car and Senna suffered a sore left thumb and forearm. Fortunately for man and machine, there was a day's respite before final qualifying. Senna spun while making a last attempt to reach the front row. He had to be satisfied with third place; a double blow because not only was arch-enemy Prost on pole, but also Schumacher had put the yellow Benetton-Ford alongside the blue Williams on the front row. Knowing he had no chance of defeating these two in a straight fight, Ayrton chose to wait for the drama that usually attends this unique race. It came sooner than expected.

Prost received a 10-second stop-go penalty for jumping the start and compounded his difficulties by stalling twice during the stop. One down; one to go.

Schumacher looked untouchable as the Benetton used traction control for the first time. The Benetton was ahead by 15 seconds when a hydraulics failure brought a devastated Schumacher to a halt. Senna's lead was such that he had time to stop for tyres, endure a delay because of a problem with the front jack and still emerge with a nine-second lead over Hill. It was to be an emotional moment for Damon, when he followed in the footsteps of his illustrious father onto the podium. At the post-race press conference, Hill paid a dignified tribute to Senna and his record sixth Monaco victory.

'I think it is as much a tribute to my father as it is to Ayrton that it has taken someone of his calibre to beat the record,' said Hill. 'If my father were still here, he would be the first to congratulate Ayrton.'

Senna reached over and grasped Hill's hand. It was a poignant moment and came as a happy follow-up to a previous exchange in the aftermath of the San Marino Grand Prix four weeks before. Angry that Hill had proved difficult to overtake and, in the process, Prost had passed them both, Senna had summoned the Englishman to his motorhome.

PEOPLE MUST HAVE
THOUGHT I WAS A
BIT NUTS WHEN
THEY SAW ME IN MY
METRO WEARING
AYRTON SENNA'S
RED FLAMEPROOF
GLOVES.
RYAN LEWIS

Damon Hill *I sort of mentioned that I was only doing what I'd seen Ayrton do many times and politely added that I didn't really think he would succeed in intimidating me in this way. There was no bad feeling or anything like that. We had never really talked before and I think he was trying to say: 'Welcome to Formula 1. If you do what I say, you'll be all right.' It all seemed a bit strange, really. Just his way of saying 'Hello' and seeing what sort of reaction he got from me.*

The Monaco result would have to sustain Senna for five months as Prost and Williams won four races in succession and extended Alain's lead of the championship. Meanwhile, McLaren were exploring all avenues in a bid to find the funds to pay their star driver and keep him on board.

Ryan Lewis

I joined the team in '93 and I was working in the clothing store. One of my jobs was to pack the drivers' kit into the drawers in the truck before the trucks left for the races. Around the middle of the year, a deal had been done with Shell and Ford which involved having their logos on the leather patches across the knuckles of Ayrton's driving gloves. These duly arrived and I put them in the drawer as usual.

On the Monday morning after the race, there was a great deal of fuss because the gloves hadn't been worn; therefore, the logos hadn't been seen from the onboard camera. I did a bit of investigating and found that Senna liked his boots and gloves worn-in so that they fitted him – like a glove! – particularly for the races. He would usually break in new boots and gloves during testing and, of course, this hadn't happened. These were brand-new gloves and he wouldn't wear them. What could I do?

I lived in Sidcup, which was over an hour's journey each way to McLaren. The only answer was for me to wear the gloves while driving my little Metro GTA to and from work every day for a week. People must have thought I was a bit nuts when they saw me in my Metro – which was red – wearing Ayrton Senna's red flameproof gloves. But it did the trick. After a week, the leather was soft rather than brand new

and tight. I put the gloves in his drawer and, at the next race, there they were, on the telly. I regret now that I never took any photographs. I was only doing my job, even though it meant my only claim to fame is that I wore Ayrton's gloves before he did.

Senna would not get to wave his gloved hand in victory for quite some time. There was to be no upturn, not even when McLaren finally received an engine of the exact same specification as Benetton, Schumacher adding to Senna's frustration by continuing to outscore the Brazilian. It was possible to sense the decline in Senna's enthusiasm in Hungary and Belgium, judging by increasingly terse comments in his press statements. McLaren personnel, intensely loyal to Senna in the past, were quietly noting that their man's motivation no longer appeared to be at its previously high level.

Meanwhile, four days after scoring his first F1 podium by finishing third at Monza, Andretti announced he was quitting F1 with immediate effect in order to give Hakkinen a race seat. 'Mika has impressed us enormously during testing but we wanted to see how he compared with Ayrton, in identical cars, at a race,' said Dennis. 'This was the only way we could find out just how good he is.'

The answer to that would be very good indeed – as a startled Senna was to discover in Portugal when he was out-qualified by a team-mate for the first time in 18 months.

Dave Ryan

This was Mika's first race for us at Estoril. Up until that point in 1993, Ayrton hadn't really been with a team-mate who made him work hard to be quicker. In fairness to Michael [Andretti], he didn't get any testing, so we never saw his true capabilities. In my opinion, Ayrton's performance level had gone down. So Michael leaves the team, Mika turns up in Portugal – and he's bloody quick. We're sitting round the table in a cramped office that night doing the debrief. We've got the traces out. Ayrton looks at the sheet and says: 'Mika, you're flat here. How are you flat there?'

Mika just stood up, put his hand on his crotch and said: 'Big balls.' Ayrton didn't say a word, got up – and walked out! He wouldn't debrief with Mika after that.

That was actually a mistake by Mika, because he really paid for it. Not only did Ayrton not tell him anything in the future, he also stepped up his pace. I'd never seen anything like it before because Ayrton really was not used to that!

The status quo would return in the race as Senna led Hakkinen until side-lined with engine trouble. The race itself was almost a subtext to a Portuguese weekend filled with significant events in the paddock. Prost, as the new champion, announced his decision to quit F1. Although Alain did not admit it at the time, this was because Williams (under pressure from Renault) had chosen to sign Senna for 1994 even though Williams and Renault knew Prost would never tolerate being in the same team as Ayrton.

There would be a frosty atmosphere on the podium at Suzuka as they stood side by side, Senna on the upper step after another virtuoso performance on a wet/ dry track. The same could not be said for his behaviour after the race, when he marched down to the Jordan office and laid into Eddie Irvine, the Ulsterman, who had finished sixth in his first Grand Prix. Along the way, on a damp track, Irvine had dared to unlap himself, a move that did not impress his senior. At the post-race press conference, Ayrton accused Irvine of 'driving like a lunatic'. Irvine later said he didn't care – or words to that effect.

This was relayed to Senna when he entered the Camel hospitality area where Berger was enjoying a glass of schnapps – and persuaded Ayrton to do the same. Being almost teetotal, the effect of the schnapps on Senna was immediate and exaggerated beyond normal bounds – as Berger knew it would. As Ayrton continued talking about Irvine's behaviour, Berger agreed with him. 'You should do something about it,' said Gerhard mischievously. Suitably fortified, Senna decided to take his friend's advice.

The subsequent interview with the less-than-contrite Irvine ended when Senna, now very angry over the lack of respect, lunged at the Jordan driver, who fell off the table he was nonchalantly sitting on and landed on the floor. This would not hurt Irvine as much as the official repercussions would affect his assailant.

A few days earlier, Williams had officially announced their new signing, Ayrton speaking to the assembled company at the team's headquarters in Didcot via a satellite link with São Paulo. There was a brisk response from Brazil to a question about the surprise news that McLaren had signed a deal with Peugeot for the supply of engines in 1994.

Mika Hakkinen soon learned not to
make jokes at Senna's expense.

Ayrton's penultimate victory at Suzuka; one
of his favourite race tracks.

'My decision [to join Williams] was made some time ago,' said Senna. 'It is
not relevant that the Peugeot deal came through'.

Dennis, meanwhile, provided an interesting slant on the subject
when discussing a telephone conversation with Ayrton three days
before the Williams announcement.

'Ayrton rang to tell me of his plans,' said Dennis. 'When I reciprocated,
telling him of our agreement with Peugeot, there was a long silence.
Perhaps he will have time to reflect on this later.'

The Peugeot deal had been unexpected, if only because McLaren had
tested an MP4/8 with a Lamborghini V12 engine in the back. Senna
had driven the car, Neil Trundle and Ron Pellat being among the test
team members looking after the project.

NOT ONLY DID
AYRTON NOT TELL
MIKA ANYTHING IN
THE FUTURE, HE
ALSO STEPPED UP
HIS PACE.
DAVE RYAN

Ron Pellat

It came to the test team as a project and several mechanics worked on it at different times. The package was fantastic; the engine, although longer than the Ford, was very neat and tidy.

We started testing with Ayrton and Mika for its first outing at Silverstone; it showed promise then. Everyone was pretty impressed with the performance and Ayrton couldn't wait to get out and try it. It was active; basically an MP4/8 but with a V12 engine that had more power than the Ford which meant the drivers could push the car a bit more.

We went to Pembrey for another test with Ayrton and Mika. Before we could run, the mechanics had to go out for a while in the hire cars to get a dry line. Then they sent Mika out, and he was rolling the tyres off the rims! That was the nature of the test; so relaxed, but everyone was up for it. The atmosphere was fantastic because the drivers loved the car. We knew if Ayrton liked this car, it had to be good. He knew what he wanted. His word counted for a lot when decisions were made; it was almost as if he was rubber-stamping this car.

The story was that the test team were going to race it in the last three races with Mika. We had Michael Andretti as our second driver at the time. We were all set. And we just knew we were going to put this car on pole.

This project was a feather in the cap for the test team because we had a product that we felt was going to beat the boys in the race team. We were kitted out in white Boss gear – except the trousers, of course. We didn't have any sponsorship; the car was all white. We practised pit stops, rehearsed everything in the pits and in the garage; we really were that far down the road.

Then, less than two weeks before going to Portugal, the project was cancelled. Why this happened, I don't know. Some people reckoned it was a pole position car but not a race winner because it probably wouldn't do a race distance. Either way, we were gutted because we were ready to go.

For me, one of the saddest things happened as we were packing up after the test. I was under the car, doing something with the floor, and Ayrton got underneath and shook my hand. He said: 'Goodbye, Ron.' That seemed very strange because normally he'd maybe shake hands or wave and say, 'See you later'. In fact, it was to be his last time with the test team. He didn't say why he was saying goodbye because he knew at that point he was going to Williams, but he couldn't say anything to us.

Indy Lall

My last test with Ayrton was in Estoril. That was really sad for me – not because we were losing an amazing racing driver to another team; that happens – but from a friendship point of view. He gave me some personal gifts; absolutely nothing major but, to this day, I still have them. It was such sad moment for me. It was like somebody leaving home.

For his final race in a McLaren, Senna would be relying on the Ford V8 as usual; it would stand him in good stead as he claimed pole and won in Adelaide. Prost finished second, the Williams being no match for a McLaren had that been refined and improved – albeit several races too late. It was a perfect way for Senna to conclude his six years with McLaren.

As if to round everything off in a satisfactory manner, Senna grabbed Prost's left wrist and dragged him onto the top level of the podium. Having studiously ignored the Frenchman in similar circumstances two weeks before in Japan, Ayrton was calling the shots and leaving Prost with no option but to accept the gesture rather than appear to be unsporting. Either way, it was a fitting end to a highly dramatic sporting contest between the two men who had more or less dominated F1 for a decade.

The beginning of the end. Senna hoists Prost's arm aloft at the end of their final race together in Australia and after turning his back on the Frenchman two weeks before in Japan.

THE WHOLE SEASON WAS AN EMOTIONAL ONE. BUT YOU COULD SEE THE TIDE START TO TURN.
RON DENNIS

Ron Dennis

The whole season was an emotional one. It had been a hard winter because of the negotiations and we were tired. The Renault was the engine to have, and I think Ayrton felt a little amount of uncertainty about the arrival of the Ford. But then you could see the tide start to turn once he drove the car and he started winning.

In fact, that was a very enjoyable period of my relationship with Ayrton. There was an element of personal satisfaction in knowing that we'd created a car that was extremely competitive; it had an unbelievable amount of attention to detail underneath the skin. At the time, it was by far the most technically advanced car we'd ever built; it was immediately quick. And, more importantly, Ayrton really loved driving it; he found the best from it very quickly.

From a racing point of view, the Donington win doesn't stand out any more than some of the others that year. A wet race is always a mentally and emotionally draining experience, and you often have nothing left on the pit wall once it's finished, so it's not a race I perhaps remember with as much clarity as some of the others.

What I do remember was the momentum we gathered through that spring, winning Brazil, Donington and at Monte Carlo. It was a fun time to go racing. It was uncomplicated, and I remember Ayrton really enjoyed it.

To mark Senna's departure from McLaren, Marlboro produced a laser disc containing highlights of their relationship. The case carried a message from Ron Dennis:

'Dear Ayrton,' it said. 'The best in anything is expensive. Occasionally, though, you get value for money. Not all of the time, but most of the time. Thanks for all the results and the good times shared. Have a nice holiday in Didcot. From one friend to another, Ron Dennis.'

The cheeky reference to a holiday at Williams hinted that Dennis reckoned Ayrton night one day return to the team that had brought all his success. Most of McLaren believed that, too. Sadly, such understandable optimism would be tragically erased six months later.

9. THE LEGACY

BEFORE IMOLA,
AYRTON CALLED
ME, NOT EVERY
DAY, BUT ALMOST.
ALAIN PROST

Ayrton goes to the grid for the last time. Imola. 1 May 1994.

Ayrton seemed preoccupied as he waited for the start of the San Marino Grand Prix. His Williams, its right-front corner missing, is returned to the pits (right).

The effect of Ayrton Senna's death was profound. The date, 1 May 1994, would become as deeply engraved on the subconscious as 7 April 1968, the day the sport lost Jim Clark in a crash at Hockenheim. Motor racing people of that era could tell you exactly where they were when the unexpected news came through from Germany. Clark was so good, he seemed indestructible, even at a time when tragedy was commonplace.

It was the same with Senna, the difference being that significant safety advances meant there had not been a fatality in a Grand Prix for 12 years. And, on this occasion, people who knew little about motor racing, but were intrigued by Senna's charisma and status as a sporting icon, would share the sport's shock and sorrow. It was, in effect, the first time such a distressing scene had been relayed to living rooms around the world.

Indy Lall *Ordinarily, we'd watch every race on television. But because this was the 1 May, it was my daughter's first birthday and we were in the garden. Someone called me in and said there had been an accident involving Ayrton. I watched it and watched it and watched it, just waiting for news. Even though I'd obviously seen far worse accidents, somehow this did not feel right. When the news came through, I was just destroyed; absolutely destroyed. I thought of so many things going across the 10 years and more that I'd known him. Above all, I remembered that last test at Estoril when he said goodbye.*

Neil Oatley *Looking back, Ayrton seemed to be fairly troubled that weekend, although we [at McLaren] wouldn't have been aware of any of that at the time. He was a mentor to Rubens [Barrichello] throughout his career and Rubens' crash during Friday-morning practice had started the weekend off in a bad way. Ayrton's push for safety on the circuits had been very much stronger than earlier in his career. That may have stemmed from [Martin] Donnelly's accident [Jerez 1990]; he was quite affected by that. Ayrton felt it more intensely than most drivers and it increased his level of safety involvement in the following seasons. Then, of course, he went to the scene of [Roland] Ratzenberger's fatal accident on the Saturday at Imola.*

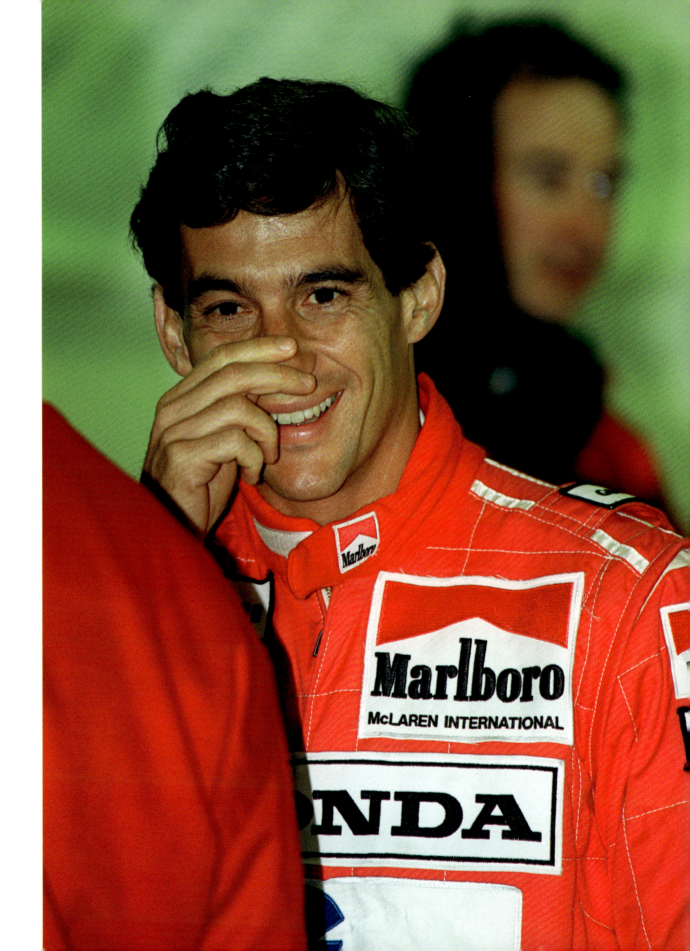

In the days and weeks that followed, McLaren personnel would support each other and be bolstered by personal memories from many different occasions and sources.

Ian 'Barney' Barnard

I had worked part-time for McLaren as a van driver and I was really keen to work there full-time. I kept my foot in the door and when I heard they were looking for someone to work in the stores, I said I would definitely go for it. I had a call from one of my mates at McLaren and he told me to submit a CV.

I didn't have a CV. It was early evening and my wife and I got out this old typewriter and eventually put something together. I was going to put it in the post but we decided to deliver it by hand that night. Having talked our way past security at the gate, I pulled up outside the dark glass entrance doors – only to discover there was no letterbox. I started to push the envelope through the gap between the doors and, suddenly, I saw movement inside, from somewhere behind the reception desk.

This person was on the phone and, still talking, as he came to the door. 'Christ!' I thought. 'That's Ayrton Senna!' I've pulled the envelope back out and he's banging on the glass telling me to try again. I did, he pulled it through – and gave a thumbs up. I got back in the car and said to my wife: 'You'll never believe this; Ayrton Senna's just taken my CV!' It was just so exciting; quite emotional, actually.

I got the job. We wouldn't see Ayrton when he was back in Brazil in the off-season. But when he did come to the factory, there was a real buzz about the place. People would be waiting to see him; that was the charisma of the man. I got to talk to him one day and told him the story of the CV. He remembered, and said he was using Ron's phone that night to call Brazil! Having met you, he never forgot your name.

I'm transport manager now but, as I said, at the time when Ayrton was with us, I worked in goods-in. The amount of stuff we used to receive from fans for Ayrton was unbelievable, particularly from Japan; things like origami birds using different-coloured paper; silk dressing gowns. Others would send him hand-made biscuits; fortune cookies; you name it. When he came to the factory, Ayrton would systematically go through everything. He never idly looked at something and threw it in the bin; he took an interest in everything. He really cared.

On one occasion, a Grateful Dead CD arrived, accompanied by a very humble letter from [lead guitarist] Jerry Garcia. His son had become an Ayrton fan and Garcia was saying he fully understood what it was to be famous and how having people write to you can be difficult. He simply said something like: 'If you have it in your heart to send me an autograph for my son, I would be incredibly grateful. And, by the way, if you haven't heard of me, I enclose one of my CDs for you.'

Ayrton looked at this CD; he hadn't got a clue who Garcia was. I told him they're one of the most iconic rock bands going. 'Really?' he said. He would write notes to himself on the back of the letter and then reply in person. He said he wasn't sure if he would like the CD, so he gave it to me. I've still got it, of course.

A GRATEFUL DEAD CD ARRIVED, ACCOMPANIED BY A VERY HUMBLE LETTER TO AYRTON FROM JERRY GARCIA. HIS SON HAD BECOME AN AYRTON FAN. AYRTON LOOKED AT THIS CD; HE HADN'T GOT A CLUE WHO GARCIA WAS.
IAN 'BARNEY' BARNARD

Caroline Whyman

I joined McLaren in March 1989, working as the team travel co-ordinator. I knew nothing about Formula 1 – at all. I had a fax machine at the end of my desk and, within about two weeks of my joining, this chap came in to use it. Being new, I had found everyone to be very friendly. So I'm chatting to this guy and, when I asked him where he worked, he burst out laughing. It was Ayrton! From that moment on, I think he was quite charmed by the fact that I had no idea who he was.

I then started to help with hospitality at the races. Whenever Ayrton saw me, it didn't matter whether he was with a group of media or busy with Ron, he would always stop and say hello. I think he liked the fact that I thought he was just another member of the team.

He was always very professional but he could be really difficult at times, there's no two ways about it. If you were getting him to do something he didn't want to do, or if something didn't quite work out or the timings weren't right for, say, the helicopter, he'd let you know for sure.

The team was smaller then and you had a much more personal relationship with the drivers than you do now. I was a nobody in the grand scheme of things but he would make the effort to say hello and he always sent me a Christmas card with a personal message; you kind of fell in love with him because of things like that. He made you feel very special when he did turn his attention to you.

We would do dinners at the races for people like Marlboro and, occasionally, I ended up sitting next to him at the table. Some people tended to avoid him because he was so intense; very serious. He almost couldn't talk about anything other than Formula 1 or his model helicopters. He wouldn't want to know anything about you, although he would often ask: 'When are you going to come and see me in Brazil?' When he left McLaren, a lot of us hadn't really accepted that he'd gone to Williams. I felt that it was all a big mistake and he'd be back.

I was working at Imola on 1 May 1994. I'd seen so many accidents when drivers just walked away, so this was a real wake-up call – particularly because it was Ayrton. For me, he was the master.

How can this happen to him? How can it? It can't be right.

Because most of us couldn't go to Brazil for the funeral, we had a memorial service in the little local church not far from the factory. That's when you remember the little things that happened. I've got paper cuttings; all the photographs over the years; the Christmas cards; you cling on to those. I've got a New Year's card looking into '94. Again, it said: 'When are you coming to see me in Brazil?' That's obviously very precious now.

Neil Trundle

Ayrton would give the appearance of being aloof; but he wasn't. That was because he was so focused. He was very sincere. When he came round the factory – we were much smaller then than we are now – he would go round every department and say hello. He'd shake hands; really grab you by the arm. It was a nice touch and meant a lot to the guys on the shop floor.

Lyndy Redding

I had started off in F1 doing catering for Ford and Leyton House before going to work for Marlboro. Initially, I was working on the tests, which in those days were much more frequent. That's when I first met Ayrton and I remember him being comparatively relaxed during most of the long tests; he would be very different at the races.

I worked in one of the Marlboro units where the kitchen was open-plan in front of a lounge area. So we would spend a lot of time hanging out during testing with Gerhard [Berger] and Ayrton; they had immense fun the whole time. Ayrton was very different to Gerhard – who was naughty and funny. Ayrton could be hugely intense, but Gerhard made him happy and helped him relax.

They would take the piss out of each other and play practical jokes. On one occasion at Monza, when they were rushing for a plane, Gerhard had put mint essence into the car's air conditioning unit; when it came through, it made them cry. But they were in a hurry and couldn't stop.

Ayrton had an aura about him. Sometimes he was so focused, he wouldn't say hello. It wasn't that he was being rude, it was because he was in a zone; totally in another place. But when he did say hello, he was just so hugely genuine; he always used to kiss us and hold our faces, which was hugely intense, but absolutely lovely. And then he would kiss us all goodbye.

When he was finally leaving McLaren, there was a feeling of absolute devastation and sadness among everybody in the team. You knew that he was definitely different to any other driver; so amazing. It was like a receiving line as he said goodbye to everybody, whereas with other drivers it would be, 'Yeah, well, that's it. Goodbye; see ya some time.'

I was at Imola in 1994. It had been a terrible weekend already with Rubens' [Barrichello] and then Roland's [Ratzenberger] accident, which affected everybody. I saw Ayrton's crash on the TV monitor. After that, I don't even remember who won. We were all crying; three girls, sitting on the back stairs that went to the roof in that unit. We went back to our hotel, which happened to be the most depressing hotel you've ever seen; brown carpet on the walls; everything was this horrible brown. And that night there was a massive thunder storm. The whole thing was like a nightmare.

They had been very happy days with all sorts of things happening. Quite often, because of sponsorship deals and so on, the badges on the drivers' overalls would change. Because we were the girls of the team, and obviously the only people who could sew, we would be handed overalls and asked to change the patches. So I used to take them back to my hotel room and sit in my bed with Ayrton Senna's overalls. Quite bizarre! But it was just one of the things you did and it is part of so many wonderful memories.

AYRTON MADE YOU FEEL VERY SPECIAL WHEN HE DID TURN HIS ATTENTION TO YOU.
CAROLINE WHYMAN

Peter Stayner

Having met Ayrton when I was manager of the Snetterton circuit during his Formula Ford days, our paths crossed again in '89 when I joined the marketing side of McLaren.

I would be involved with appearances and interviews at the race, so I got to know him quite well there. He had obviously changed out of all recognition from the quiet, shy guy who didn't speak much English in the early 1980s. Now he was someone very special; he had a great deal of presence.

When we went to these sponsor functions, he was nearly always late because he'd been having long discussions with the engineers at the track. It might be a Marlboro or a Shell function with 150 guests waiting with great expectation. There were no mobile phones then, so you might not be able to warn them that he was running late. I remember one particular occasion in a big theatre complex in Brazil and the audience was pretty restless. Ayrton went straight onto the stage – and the whole room fell silent. It was like royalty arriving. Immediately, he had them in the palm of his hand. He could have read the Yellow Pages and they wouldn't have cared; they loved him. He had this immaculate presence and he knew how to handle people.

He could also be difficult if he didn't want to do a function. He'd say, 'Peter, I don't think I should do this.' I would say, 'But it's on the schedule, Ayrton. We've approved it; you've got to do it.' 'No,' he'd say. 'I don't think so.' In the end, he would do it; he was just playing with you a little bit. But once he was there, he was superb.

Alain Prost

When I retired, we saw a new Ayrton Senna. Looking back, ours is a fantastic story in sport, one that only happens, I don't know, 4 or 5 times in 50 years. It was good for F1 and kept it in on the front pages. We keep it in people's memories because we were the human part; we had characters. Before Imola, Ayrton called me, not every day, but almost. There's a few things he told me that I would never tell anyone. I would never tell anything about what he said during this week; it's in my heart. I would like everyone to know who Ayrton Senna was. He was a different person when racing against me; it was not like when he was fighting against Michael [Schumacher] or Nigel [Mansell] or whoever. Fighting against me, he was different and I don't have any problem with that now. He wanted to beat me. I have to thank him because, when we were team-mates, we drove each other on. But our story did not end in 1994. Our story will last … forever.

The most profound and far-reaching aspect of his life has been the Ayrton Senna Foundation, which quickly gathered momentum in 1994 to become a powerful cause for good in Brazil – just as Ayrton would have wished.

Bianca Lalli

In January and February of 1994, Ayrton and my mother had talked about doing something. Very soon after the funeral, my mother talked to us about it, saying it was his wish to do something for Brazil in a professional way. He had done a lot for Brazil beforehand but he wanted something more structured; more professional. He had asked my mother to think about what that could be but he never got the chance to decide what could be done. He had the dream; we knew the feeling that he wanted this.

We decided to create the foundation. He really loved children; he always said that children are the future of the world and we needed to do things for them. This is how we have connected his dream to do something for Brazil and for children. Everything happened really, really quickly. My mother didn't want to wait; it was almost like a means of helping her cope with the whole thing.

Bruno Senna

One of things that Ayrton was very quick to realise was that he only achieved what he achieved because of the opportunity he had in his life.

He was privileged enough in Brazil to have access to education, to basic things like food and water, and he could develop his potential with the funding from my grandparents. What he saw in Brazil was poverty and bad situations that were not allowing people to have this chance. He was trying to give money to charity but he could never see how the work was being done, or if the money was being used properly. So he thought about taking it into his own hands to help people have the opportunities to be the best they could be. That's where the idea came from but, unfortunately, he didn't see the foundation coming together.

Ayrton was very fond of being with the family; I knew that from the experiences we had with him personally, but also from the letters he used to send to my grandparents when he moved to England and raced in Formula Ford and F3. He would write all the time, explaining what was going on because, of course, at that time there was not the easy access we have today to communication technology. He would explain every detail. That was the kind of person he was; trying to share everything he achieved with the family.

For us as nephews and nieces, he loved being with kids. We were the only kids he could be around and it was like we were his own. Whenever he came back from Japan to Brazil, he would bring a few bits and pieces from Japan. He was always thinking about the family, even when he was not with the family. That was very special considering how intense and how tough he was on the sporting side. It was a very interesting contrast for us to see.

WE REMEMBER
THE EXCEPTIONAL
VALUES HE HAD;
THE PRINCIPLES
HE WORKED
AND LIVED BY.
SIMPLY PUT, WE
REMEMBER AN
EXTRAORDINARY
HUMAN BEING.
RON DENNIS

Viviane Lalli

Ayrton would always come home when he had gaps in his agenda. He loved being with our family; with my son and daughters. It was a time where he could relax and immediately be himself without having to worry about anything. It was so different from when he was at the race; he was relaxed and always smiling when he was with us. We would like to think he would feel very proud about everything that has been done in his name with the Ayrton Senna Foundation. If he was with us today, he would be very much a part of it.

Ron Dennis

When I think of Ayrton, I think of the fun we had, particularly when Gerhard was in the team. You might expect me to say I think of all the wins we had. But we were doing our job; we were there to win the races. I'm often asked what was it about Ayrton that made him great. The thing that stands out is that he was so good for the entire time he was with us. You didn't see any decline. There are quite a few drivers who stay in the sport too long and their reputation becomes tarnished. Obviously, we'll never know if that might have applied to Ayrton because all we remember is he was unbelievably competitive and then, suddenly, he wasn't there any more. Who knows what he would be like now. Obviously, he would be older, just like the rest of us, and have other things in his life. Perhaps something could have occurred that might have detracted from his reputation. But that's not what happened. His life came to an abrupt end and we remember the greatness. We remember the exceptional values he had; the principles he worked and lived by. Simply put, we remember an extraordinary human being.

INDEX

ACKNOWLEDGEMENTS

I am indebted to members of McLaren Racing, past and present, who took time to pass on their personal memories of Ayrton Senna. Thanks to: Tyler Alexander, Ian Barnard, Gerhard Berger, Ron Dennis, Osamu Goto, Mark Hannawin, Indy Lall, Ryan Lewis, Tim Murnane, Gordon Murray, Neil Oatley, Alain Prost, Lyndy Redding, Dave Ryan, Peter Stayner, Neil Trundle, John Watson, Caroline Whyman.

I would also like to thank Nigel Moss, Matt Bishop and Steve Cooper for their valuable assistance behind the scenes at the McLaren Technology Centre. And also Steve Small, Matthew Minter, Linda Keen, Max Mosley, Martin Donnelly, David Luxton, Damien Smith, the late Professor Sid Watkins and the team at Blink Publishing for their help in various ways.

I must also pay grateful tribute to the late Russell Bulgin, who kindly entrusted me with his personal interviews with Ayrton Senna and from which I have drawn heavily.

Finally, and not least, special thanks to Viviane Senna Lalli, Bruno Senna and Bianca Lalli, whose support and approval has been invaluable.

Maurice Hamilton

Bibliography

Team Lotus: My View from the Pit Wall, by Peter Warr (Haynes)
Ayrton Senna: The Whole Story, by Christopher Hilton (Haynes)
Autosport; *Autocar*; *Autocourse*; *Motor Sport*

BLINK
bringing you closer

Published by Blink Publishing
Deepdene Lodge
Deepdene Avenue
Dorking RH5 4AT, UK

www.blinkpublishing.co.uk

www.facebook.com/blinkpublishing
twitter.com/blinkpublishing

ISBN: 978-1-90582-587-5

A CIP catalogue record of this book is available from the British Library.

Design by www.envydesign.co.uk

Printed and bound in the United Kingdom by Butler, Tanner & Dennis Ltd

Colour reproduction by Aylesbury Studios Ltd.

1 3 5 7 9 10 8 6 4 2

McLaren © 2014
Text written by Maurice Hamilton 2014
Text © Blink Publishing

Pictures selected by Blink Publishing

Papers used by Blink Publishing are natural, recyclable products made from wood grown in sustainable forests. The manufacturing processes conform to the environmental regulations of the country of origin.

Every reasonable effort has been made to trace copyright holders of material reproduced in this book, but if any have been inadvertently overlooked the Publishers would be glad to hear from them

Blink Publishing is an imprint of the Bonnier Publishing Group
www.bonnierpublishing.co.uk